STRANGE ALTARS

By MARCUS BACH

Doc Reser explaining a Voodoo service as the author takes notes.

STRANGE ALTARS

by

MARCUS BACH

THE BOBBS-MERRILL COMPANY, INC.

PUBLISHERS

INDIANAPOLIS · NEW YORK

First Edition

Library of Congress Catalog Card Number: 52-10690

STRANGE ALTARS

Chapter 1

THE NIGHT BEFORE I MET HIM I heard a drum. Far away and faint, the muffled throb was the beating of the jungle's heart. I was conscious of something more than the deep vibration of sound. There was a feeling of the primitive past blending with the present, an allurement reaching back into the unknown and out to me, beckoning in a pulsing rhythm that never changed.

This was the first I had heard—a lonely drum with a lonely soul that chanted, "Come to *me,* come to *me, come* to *me!*" Two unaccented beats and one sharply accented, with a hollow, haunting quiver of suspense. I started toward the shadowy hills over which the moon was spreading a shimmering path for the climbing.

It was nine-thirty. I had been walking for some time along the Rue Grégoire in Port-au-Prince. Lured by the beat of the drum I said to myself, Isn't this always the way? Just today, after a week of fruitless searching, I learn about the one white man in Haiti who can get me into Voodoo services. Now it seems I will not need him.

The thought thrilled me with adventure. Loitering groups of black people in the darkened spaces along the street stopped

7

speaking as I approached. I gave them the magical greeting, the polite, *"Bonsoir."* There was always the inevitable response, *"Bonsoir, m'sieur,"* soft as the night air.

I knew no Creole, the patois spoken by Haiti's more than three million inhabitants, but just now I no longer felt like an intruder. The drum was a solid link between their tradition and my research.

Ever since I had stepped from the plane at the airport I had been possessed by uncertainty. I had felt small and vulnerable. The mountains and the people were the strong forces. Both had stubbornly withstood my attempts to follow a call that was neither real nor clear. What did they hold, the mountains and the people? What was behind them? What was the hidden spirit speaking warningly to my spirit, telling me that Haiti is different, that its mood cannot be fathomed or described, that its air is full of sorcery and its welcome is a spell?

For fifteen years I had been tramping the Americas in a search for meaning behind the things people believe. My quest had taken me among seemingly strange groups: the Snake Handlers in Kentucky and Tennessee, the "self-crucifiers" in New Mexico, the Trappist monks in monasteries across the United States, the Doukhobors in Canada, the Hutterites in Montana and South Dakota, the Maya-Quichés in Guatemala. Among the strange and the exotic I felt at home. Their devotion was mine, viewed and enjoyed vicariously. Their claims of an ultimate truth were my faltering hopes made visible and graphic. The sacrificial paths they walked, amazing to me but never weird, fantastic but never fanatical, were alive with spoors that urged me on.

Now for the first time in my years of investigation I realized that I was in the minority. For once I was out of place because I was white. All doors were closed. All answers to my questions were evaded. All letters of introduction were useless. But now, the telltale sound of the drum—an invitation coming unexpectedly out of the night.

The smell of a charcoal fire and the scent of flowers, the rising moon and a silent cemetery wall, a stark cross and the outline of dark faces, the murmuring incantation of the drum gave me the secure impression that I had finally mounted the stage that is Haiti. Just now I felt that I would not hesitate to travel the country's ten thousand square miles with *Bonjour* to guide me by day and *Bonsoir* by night.

I would not need the man, the strange white man whose name had been entrusted to me. I would be my own guide. The real thrill of my work was finding out the truth of things for myself, looking honestly at strange altars, gaining entrance to guarded sanctuaries, being invited as the drum invited me now with its unchanging and enchanted voice, "Come to *me*, come to *me*, come to *me!*"

I reached the somber edge of the hill and started up a winding path. The hollow detonation of the drum came from somewhere behind me. Confused, I went back. I walked to the cemetery wall, for now the sound seemed to come from inside. I went in using the cross as a guide only to find the elusively weird notes swinging back to where I thought they had been at first. The pattern never varied, the rhythm never ceased, phantom hands on a phantom drum kept repeating, "Come to *me*, come to *me!*"

The moon sprang into view with a light that was intense. It flung its halos upon the trees, brought another dimension to the spindly wooden homes and transformed the ageless cemetery into the city foursquare. It laid a silver coating across the long, irregular rows of sepulchers and gave each line and form a ghostly counterpart. In a near-by yard a rooster crowed. Farther off, a pack of dogs raised wailing cries. From distant Port-au-Prince came faintly the honking of horns, the obbligato to traffic, which never ceases day or night. But always in the hushed moment I heard the drum.

Set back against a hill was a wooden house with a long, sheltered lane leading up to it. Within the yard candles burned uncertainly. As I started toward their flickering light the throbbing drum was an echo of the pounding of my heart. I was finally touching the secret of the land, the secret that sharpens one's impulses and deepens one's sense of perception. I was coming close to the source of the power and the spirit which pervade the island. I was moving in the magnetic orbit of Voodoo, and the hypnotic sound swelled suddenly in warning.

A figure emerged from the shadows. In the moonlit circle of light stood a gaunt, thin-faced man. He was barefoot and dressed in the loose-fitting garb of a peasant. A cigarette burned in his black, almost invisible fingers. He raised his hand and smiled.

"Bonsoir, m'sieur," he greeted.

"Bonsoir."

Then in a rush of Creole and a series of impatient gestures he motioned me away.

I groped for a Creole phrase. *"Fe plezi*—if you please—*le tambour*—the drum! I heard *le tambour!"*

He waved both hands in front of my face and shook his head. In rapid cadences he impressed on me that he understood not a word of anything I could possibly say! I could venture no farther. What I hoped for could not be expressed. What I felt meant nothing to him. I finally nodded submissively with the one word all Haiti understands: "Okay." He folded his arms and grinned good-naturedly. Then he noticed that his cigarette was about to burn his fingers. I offered him one.

"*Merci, m'sieur,*" he said and accepted it. He lighted it from the stub, inhaled sharply and blew a wisp of smoke to the sky. He nodded approvingly.

The staccato tattoo of the drum, so near I felt I could reach out and touch it, beckoned beseechingly, kept up its cry, "Come to *me,* come to *me!*"

I tried once more: "*Fe plezi, m'sieur ...*"

He shook his head. His face was stern.

We stood together separated by the barrier of language. We were held apart by thoughts that could not quite make themselves known. There was no antagonism, only a sense of futility, a hopelessness of understanding either our words or our beliefs. Our eyes met across this gulf, and he stated quietly, "*Alé, zami, alé.*"

That much Creole I understood. "Go, friend, go."

I extended my hand. "*Merci.*"

He laughed spontaneously, took me by the arm and made sure I went to the end of the path. With a gracious gesture he spoke his "*Au revoir, m'sieur.*"

The echo of the drums covered the hills.

I walked away wondering about Voodoo and its closed doors. Was it possible that black is black and white is white and that there could be no crossing the cultural line?

One man had crossed it and again I thought of him. His

name seemed more vivid than it had an hour ago: Stanley Reser. I had been told that he was the one man whom the black people of Haiti trusted and loved. He alone, among the three thousand whites on the island, had got behind the faces and the forms, behind the mountains and the jungle, behind the laughter and the shadows, the poverty, pain and glory, into the spirit of the people. He, I had been assured, knew where the drums were beating and why.

"If he likes you," my informant had promised, "he can do more for you in two months than you can do on your own in Haiti in two years."

I was determined that he should like me, and I prepared to meet him early in the morning with my most pleasant *bonjour*.

2.

AT EIGHT o'clock on the following day I hailed a cab near the plaza of the Hotel Excelsior.

"Parlez-vous l'anglais?" I asked the driver.

He replied magnanimously, *"M'sieur,* I spick English a li'l bitch!"

I engaged him. He honked three times to a passer-by and took off. Like most cabbies in the city he had a habit of shutting off his motor to save gas, and he proudly called my attention to his skill in this technique. He wanted me to observe how he could cut off the motor and cut it back on with hardly a jerk. His name was Freddie.

The streets of Port-au-Prince were already a midway festive with a calliope of honking horns to which my driver added his generous part. The scene was sharply lighted by a sun which absorbed every color excepting the intense black of the people. They belonged. Proud, stoical women unconcernedly balanced heavily packed wicker baskets on their heads. They carried everything: live chickens, turkeys, fruit, garden stuff, sisal, charcoal, calabashes, wooden crates. A young girl steadied a basketful of eggs on her head. I caught sight of a boy, not more than eight, struggling under a small sack of cement with a can of water perched on top. A bicycle rider deftly balanced a huge basket loaded with green peppers. Burros laden with charcoal and burros with huge water jars lashed to their skinny flanks were guided along by men with sticks. Workmen pushed rickety carts along the open gutters. Trinket vendors, stubbornly holding their places in the moving throng, added a carnival touch. A rawboned woman, hunched upon her burro, disdained to get out of our way despite our incessant honking. She sat as comfortably as if she were in a rocker, listlessly holding a stick in her thin, black hands. Glistening sheaves of red and yellow sisal hemmed her in.

The one- and two-story business places which rose abruptly from the street were overshadowed by the black inhabitants of this teeming world. I became aware that the people represented a variety of shades from ebony-black to olive-tan. Their blood as well as their language was a patois, a mixture of Spanish, French, African. Rarely was there the intrusion of a *blanc,* but whenever I saw one I felt again the problem that confronted me. For I, too, was a *blanc,* a white outsider, wanting to get into the deepest beliefs of these natives, into the most guarded secrets of their faith, whatever that faith might be. Rhythm as well as color wove them into a common pattern. Their gait was a free and swinging tempo that put them in tune with a power that lightened their loads.

Rhythm was in the march of the guards as we passed the gleaming white Palais Nacional of the president. It was in the people who crossed the open plazas and in the slender khaki-clad men who directed traffic from under canopies in the street. It was in the cry of *Ge-e-e-a-a-a-z* of the girls who carried wooden trays with cans of kerosene on their heads. Rhythm was in the gentle sway of the sea as we reached the turn at the Rue Republicain and saw the blue water of the Caribbean. It was in the cavalcade of moving figures as we drove westward on Bizoton Road and in the air as we left the ballet of the city behind. To get at the nature and source of this symphony would require all the weeks and months I had planned for my Haitian stay. Rhythm was to Port-au-Prince what the tempo of traffic is to New York.

"Freddie," I asked, "do you know Mr. Reser at the Chez Pauline?"

He turned, somewhat startled.

"Stanley Reser?" I repeated.

His eyes grew large. *"You* know Doc Reser?" he asked. "Doc Reser my good fren. Doc Reser a big fren. Doc Reser such a big fren I take you for nothing to Chez Pauline." And he did.

When he let me out at the gate and noticed that I had left two dollars on the seat he honked three times and drove off shouting a joyful, *"Merci, m'sieur!"*

I opened the imposing iron gate to the thickly wooded grounds, and the clank of the metal latch disturbed the hush of the surroundings. A flagstone path led through an exotic tangle of shrubs and trees and gave me the pleasant sensation of being in a jungle which man had encroached on but had not conquered.

The place was a fairyland with roses and hibiscus and jasmine tucked away among mango and breadfruit trees. Blending into this perfume-scented path was the fresh fragrance of orange blossoms. Banana groves lurked deeper within, and countless tropical plants formed deep green barriers, with an occasional majestic palm reaching out for a place in the sun.

Birds chirped and fluttered in this luxuriant sanctuary. The sharp scent of the flowers became more acute as I walked on. It could hardly have been more fragrant here during those long-gone days when Pauline Bonaparte Leclerc strode impatiently through these grounds, wondering if the General could kill off enough blacks to make her life secure.

That was a hundred and fifty years ago, in the time of Christophe and Dessalines and Toussaint L'Ouverture. *"Nègres sauvages"* the arrogant French called these black men. Yet these were the great ones who became Haiti's national heroes, the liberators, the generals who embodied a spirit that never died.

Who were these men? Henri Christophe, a slave who became a king, built the majestic Citadel at Cap Haïtien, a symbol of defiance against aggression. Jean Jacques Dessalines, a slave who became a mighty general and in May 1803 tore the white out of the French flag. Toussaint L'Ouverture, a slave who became governor general of Saint Domingue. This was the trio which shared the immortal dream that the island might someday be free. The French had cannon and ships; *they* had machetes and their bare hands. These were the *"gros Nègres"* whose followers could not get it through their heads that the Christians' God was bigger or better than, or even different from, their Congo deities. While the French drank wine and knelt beneath a cross in the name of Christ, they drank *clairin* and prayed to Damballa.

I reached a clearing and stood in the cathedral stillness of the surroundings. The perfumed air was incense. Trees were the vaulted ceilings. The sun came through with the softness of a votive light.

Before me was a large stone barn, across whose gable was printed, "Leclerc, brother-in-law of Napoleon Bonaparte, general of the French armies, born at Pontoise, died here of yellow fever in 1802." Near by was another building that looked deserted. Around it were statues of the nine muses. A swimming pool with its gargoyles and Janus-faced figures was dust-dry. A recumbent statue of Pauline, weathered and forlorn, was all that remained to show she had once wanted to be Empress of Haiti—or rather, Empress of Saint Domingue, for in those days the entire island, now divided between the Dominican Republic and Haiti, was one stake in the planned conquest of the French. Only the statues remained. Only a gardener's hand held back the creeping jungle.

"Bonjour!"

I turned and met the pleasantly dreamy gaze of a young Haitian who stood not more than ten feet from me. He was leaning lazily on the handle of his homemade broom as if he had been watching me for some time. He was in his mid-twenties, lightly dressed and wearing loose-fitting sandals.

"You look for someone, *m'sieur?"* he asked in English.

"Doctor Reser."

"Ah!" It was his way of saying, "I understand." Then he asked, "He knows you?"

"No. Is he here?"

"You wait, please," he said, propping the broom against a tree. "I am Diogène. I go and see."

He walked toward a small, vine-covered cottage. Reser, I had been told, lived here alone, apart from the white colony of Port-au-Prince. He was the present overseer of the estate, but rarely was he seen at functions of the elite. There were rumors that he was a confirmed recluse. It was also said that some years ago he had been forced to decide between returning to the States with his wife and two children or remaining in Haiti. He chose the Magic Isle. His stay was now in its twenty-fifth year. No one knew too much about his past; no one spoke freely of his present life or work. Everyone tacitly agreed that he was a "different kind of *blanc*," and shrugged mysteriously.

Diogène came from the house and beckoned to me. He held open the door, meanwhile speaking softly in Creole to someone inside.

At a small round table sat a strongly built man eating breakfast. He glanced up as I paused in the doorway.

"It's all right," he said reassuringly. "Sit down."

The extra chair at the table might have been set there for my coming. I introduced myself. He repeated my name as if fixing it forever in his mind.

It was difficult to figure him out. His straight-featured, unwrinkled face, bronzed by the Caribbean sun, suggested a man of forty-five or fifty. I had been told he was sixty-three. He could have been Irish or Indian or German. He was, however, an American of Scandinavian descent, with thinning blond hair which had a touch of gray. The firm set of the jaw, the muscular arms and shoulders showing through the thin white shirt hinted that he had known hard manual labor. One thing I noticed particularly—a red-and-green dragon vividly tattooed on his right arm.

Something marked him as different from other men, an inner self-assurance in which a number of personalities held the stage, each directed by the visible man, the man who now ate slowly, tasting to the full every bite of a luscious yellow-red mango and contemplating every sip of milk from the tall glass.

He smacked his lips. "Coconut milk," he said. "Care for some? Have you had breakfast?"

I assured him I had.

"Well, have some milk."

He clapped his hands and called sharply, "André!"

Diogène, who stood in the open doorway, moved aside as a handsome olive-skinned boy in his late teens came into the room.

Now for a moment I heard and saw another Reser emerge from within the mysterious regiment of characters which I had sensed in him. This one announced himself in a flood of Creole. His eyes sprang into expressive light. His face appeared almost Negroid. He spoke with both voice and hands.

The youth stood at attention, his face registering keen delight as if he were hearing some half-forgotten story. At the finish he broke into spontaneous laughter and ran happily from the room.

This brief interlude gave me my first insight into Reser's undeniable oneness with the native people. He spoke their language as though it were his mother tongue, and he caught the mood and rhythm which were theirs. By some deft genius he was both master and friend, and there was no question about his ability as a raconteur.

Returning again to the role of host, he said genially, "Just a little folk story about a man who came to dinner."

I took note of my surroundings. From the sparse furnishings my gaze traveled to the whitewashed walls where colored sketches of Haitian people and native scenes were hung. An improvised shelf held books on philosophy, medicine and art. Then, through the partially curtained doorway, I saw in the adjoining room three drums, graduated in size, slender and round, with pegs holding down the taut drumheads.

"Voodoo," said my host before I realized he was watching me. "Voodoo drums."

André, with a graceful gliding motion, came in with the milk.

"That's why I came to you, Doctor Reser," I began. "Voodoo."

He shrugged.

"The truth about Voodoo," I said earnestly.

He did not reply.

"I don't think the truth about it has ever been told," I insisted. "Do you think so?"

He looked at me questioningly.

André brought a package of cigarettes and some matches and laid them before us. Reser thanked him with a glance. Then with a word of command he dismissed the two house boys and sat for a time smoothing a cigarette between his fingers.

"The truth about Voodoo?" He smiled dubiously. "Are you sure you want it? There is a Congo proverb, 'If you don't want the gun to go off, don't cock the trigger.'"

"Who is the gun?" I asked with a laugh. "You or Voodoo?"

"A good question," he said seriously. He struck a match on

the bottom of his chair and lighted his cigarette. "You mean to say," he queried, "that a white man can ever know the truth about Voodoo?"

"I am told that *you* know it."

"I do." His reply was final.

"Aren't you white?" I asked.

This amused him. "Some years ago," he recalled, "when I was in north Haiti with the American Medical Corps I went to several Voodoo services. One of my associates said, 'Reser, white men do not fraternize with the blacks.' I said, 'But I do.' My associate said, 'My statement still stands!'"

With this equivocal remark he leaned back in his chair and began to quiz me on my research. His interest grew as I recounted my experiences among various groups, and he was apparently impressed, for he became warmly talkative. His knowledge of the wide variety of religious and folk traditions was astonishing. He questioned me in detail on Rosicrucianism and New Thought and went into intimate detail in a discussion of many philosophical and religious movements. He encouraged me to tell him more about the Kingdoms of Father Divine and the claims of the various holiness groups. He spurred me on to talk about the Swedenborgians, the Vedantists, the followers of the Baha'i faith, the Christian Scientists and the Theosophists. My mention of spiritualism called up another Reser, a master metaphysician and eschatologist. He knew the field, the history and the phenomena. He was acquainted with modern mediums, and he knew as well as anyone I had ever met the "spiritualism of the Scriptures."

He became so engrossed in the subject that he switched to French, which he spoke as fluently as Creole, then to Spanish

and frequently lost me in this trilingual shuffle. His cigarette
burned itself out. He took another, scratched a match on the
bottom of the chair and inquired, "By the way, who told you
about me?"

"A man at the American Embassy," I said. "John Campbell,
head of the Department of Humanities."

"I see. I thought perhaps you had seen my name in *Life*
magazine."

"A story about you?"

"I was mentioned in connection with a very dear friend of
mine," he explained. "He passed on a short time ago. Cicéron."
He repeated the name as if trying to call him back from
the dead. "Cicéron was our greatest drummer. Haiti's greatest
drummer," he corrected. "His hands were gnarled from years
of playing. The heel of his hand had great cushions—calluses.
His thumbs were enlarged to nearly twice their normal size."
He looked at his hands as he spoke.

It seemed to me that his thumbs were enlarged, too, and that
the heels of his hands were callused. "Do you play the drums?"
I asked.

"Why, of course. Naturally. What a question!"

I now saw a man delighted with an inner experience, boyishly
contemplating secrets that were jealously withheld from chance
acquaintances, stirred by memories that were roguishly saying,
If you only knew!

He continued in a solemn tone. "Cicéron once made a drum
for me. He dug a hole in the ground, put in the piece of oak as if
he were setting a post. Then he grubbed out the inner core by
chopping and digging. This took several days. Later he covered the top with a select piece of cowhide. Goat hides are used

for Martinique and work drums, cowhides for Rada drums. Those are Rada drums in there. The hides are softened up with *clairin* and egg yolk. Then comes the ceremony of dedication. A man never forgets this. The drums often bear signs and symbols which have great meaning."

"What kind of signs? What kind of symbols?"

"Voodoo," he answered. "But Voodoo is not understood through symbols and signs. It is understood through the people. The women in the market places, the men in the fields, the peasants in the mountains where the white man does not go, the people on the plantations whom the white man does not see, the priest and the priestess whose secrets the white man does not know, the children who learn the prayers along with their names and who—thank God!—have not been corrupted by the white man's sense of values. To know Voodoo is to know the people, three and a half million of them, in this the first free black republic on the face of the earth."

"All Voodooists?"

"Not all, but the majority, especially the country people. Oh, there are a few among the elite, but the elite seldom attend the ceremonies. They are just as ignorant of real Voodoo as are the tourists. Some of them know about it and avoid it. They say, 'That is the affair of the peasant with whom I have nothing in common.' Good. We have a proverb, 'The affairs of the sheep are not the affairs of the goats.' So be it."

"But Voodoo *is* a religion?"

"If not, what is it?" The answer was emphatic. "It has its priests and priestesses."

"How many?"

"I can't say."

"A hundred?"

"More than that. And it has its places of worship, its rites, its beliefs, its faith and its power. Great faith and great power, power to do things which other religions claim to do but never demonstrate."

"You have been in Voodoo a long time?"

He gave me a quick glance as though to answer, but instead he rose impulsively.

"What do you expect to find down here, anyway?" he asked.

"I have no preconceived ideas," I parried.

"Oh, yes, you have. Everyone has who comes to Haiti."

"I have none that cannot be changed if the facts warrant."

He looked at me searchingly. "In the religions you have studied, what have you found? What do you believe?"

"I believe," I told him, "that when men really find the great thing, the pearl of great price, it is one and the same no matter in which faith they find it."

Slowly he ground out his cigarette. "The pearl of great price," he said with emotion. "And Haiti is the Black Pearl of the Caribbean. When one has found both of these . . . ah, yes, yes." He took a deep breath and went on with a rising sense of warmth. "Voodoo is a power which cannot be analyzed unless you believe. I cannot take you into Voodoo. Voodoo works from within. There are secrets in the practices which those on the outside never know and those on the inside never reveal."

"That," I had to say, "is true of most religious groups and most fraternal orders. Isn't that true of Masonry?"

He looked at the ring he was wearing. "Yes," he observed with a smile, "I suppose it is."

Now for the first time he seemed completely friendly. He

extended his hand to me. As we gripped hands he surprised me by saying, "You have come to me at a good time. I am not doing anything special for the next four or five weeks. What do you say we look at Haiti together?"

"Wonderful! And Voodoo?"

"Well," he said, "you cannot separate the people from their beliefs any more than you can separate the mind from its thoughts. And you cannot take away the pearl of great price from the one who has found it."

"There is just one other matter, Doctor Reser," I said. "My wife is with me here in Haiti. I hope it will be all right for her to come along when we start our research. She is the photographer on our expedition. We want to get some pictures of Voodoo services. A documentary."

My host was suddenly a stranger. His face showed resentment and evident regret that he had committed himself ever to be my guide.

"Pictures," he said in a brittle tone, "are *out*. Would you want someone coming into your church with a camera? Furthermore, Haitians have their superstitions just as other people do. Voodooists have their fears and their beliefs like anyone else. They have a feeling that if you take their picture you are capturing something spiritual, psychical, something that is part of their inner life, and you are running away with it in the little black box. Maybe they are right."

"I shall respect your opinion," I told him. "I can see that you have a deep affection for these people."

"Affection!" he exclaimed with a slight cry. "Why, man, Haiti has given me her heart. Surely the least I can do is to give my heart to Haiti."

3.

WHEN I reported Reser's ban on the picture project to Lorena she said exactly what I had expected her to say: "Let me talk to him."

There was a reason for this beyond the instinctive feminine confidence that she could bring him around to her point of view. This was her first research trip with me. I had previously gone alone, but through the years her photography had grown from a hobby to a profession, and we had agreed that we ought to team up in this Haitian venture.

She had done more than her part since we arrived in Port-au-Prince. In fact, she had started her pictorial commentary the moment we took off from the Camagüey, Cuba, airport. She had taken aerial shots of the Windward Passage, of our first glimpse of the Magic Isle, of the pink spires of the cathedral and of the gleaming white palace of the president. She had already photographed Haiti's greatest professional dancer, Destiné, and had she been with me when I heard the drum she would no doubt have tried to get a picture of the lone watchman on the lonely path. She had learned one Creole phrase, *"Quitte um tiré portré ou?"* (Please may I take your picture?)

Armed with this she had gone on daily excursions. Evenings, when she returned to the Hotel Excelsior where we had our room, she would crawl into the large wardrobe chest. This was her darkroom. I would lock the door and drape blankets over it to keep out the moonlight and then lie on the bed listening to the steady squeak of the developing tank, listening to the roosters crowing, listening to the dogs howling far off, listening for the drum until she signaled that another batch of negatives was ready for washing. I was always glad to have the signal. It at least assured me she hadn't suffocated inside the chest.

So how could I refuse her when she said, "Let me talk to him"? And how could I contradict her when she said, "If he is interested in painting, he must be interested in photography. He sounds to me like a very interesting and understanding man, even if he is an escapist."

This was exactly her frame of mind when, on the following morning at nine o'clock, I led her up the flagstone path through the grounds of the Chez Pauline.

When we reached the clearing the air was fragrant with an aroma of coffee and the pungent smell of burning pitch pine. An open charcoal fire glowed near the small kitchen some distance from Reser's house.

Diogène was slowly and rhythmically sweeping the patio. He waved a hand. "Go in," he greeted. "Doctor Reser expects you."

"Expects us?" I said in a puzzled voice.

"Well," Lorena said jokingly, "you said he was psychic!"

Reser stood in the doorway. *"Bonjour!"* he greeted.

"Bonjour, M'sieur Docteur!" I answered. "I hope we aren't disturbing you so early in the day."

"You are just in time," he said with a sweep of his hand toward the table. And when we got in I noticed there were places set for three, and André stood by with folded hands, smiling happily.

I felt immediately that Lorena and Reser would get along famously. She was fascinated by his graciousness, thinking, no doubt, that he would be a much easier touch than I had predicted, and she was already seeing photographic possibilities in André. Then, too, Reser was in a jovial mood, pleased, it seemed to me, that his hunch about our coming had been correct. He was delighted with the autographed book I brought him, and he may also have been relieved that Lorena had not shown up with a battery of cameras strung over her shoulders.

He gave André several rapid instructions, and Lorena sensed, as I had, the change in his personality when he switched to Creole. He then asked us to take places, explaining that this was to be our introduction to a typical Haitian breakfast. Evidently he was assuming that we had not eaten before we came.

As André brought the food in his graceful gliding motion Reser explained in detail how it had been prepared and defined its place in the Haitian diet.

"André usually serves me coffee in bed at about six," he said. "Then I have a hearty breakfast at eight, a habit I got into during my days on the coffee plantation. Now this is an omelet with shallots and tomatoes. Here is *yam guinea* and here I prepared just a bit of goat meat with *piment bouc*. . . ."

"You prepared it?" Lorena asked.

"Certainly! Haitian cuisine is one of my hobbies."

We started to eat. Goat meat, omelet, *yam guinea,* plantain, biscuits, coconut milk.

"This," said Reser buoyantly, "is how we suffer in Haiti!"

He was the enthusiastic gourmet, the ideal host, and to Lorena's delight went into a thorough dissertation on Haitian food. I was learning that whenever Reser entered into a subject he never got out until he had exhausted it. This was true whether he was discussing food or philosophy.

"I remember one occasion," he was saying, "when I invited

two American doctors and their wives to dine with me. This was while I was superintendent of the institution for the insane at Pont Beudet. I brought in a cook from the central plain. She knew no English. She had never lived in the city. She had never worked for anyone, but she had an instinctive talent for good food. She cooked by inspiration."

"I'd like to meet her," said Lorena.

"Oh, you can't lure her to the States," he warned with a laugh. "No true Haitian wants to leave Haiti. I know *I* don't! But about this dinner. I had prepared an appetizer of fruit juices, grenadine and corosol. Cécile, the cook, followed it with a salad of hearts of artichoke and palm, served with a sauce of mayonnaise and ketchup, beaten to a light pink. To this was added a touch of Worcestershire sauce and peanut butter. The flavor of the peanut butter was barely perceptible. *Ai-yai-yai!* The blending of tastes was indescribable!"

Lorena was interested for two reasons. She was sincerely enthusiastic about Haitian cuisine, and she knew that every word of this conversation was bringing her closer to the man she intended to sell on her picture project.

She urged him on. "What was the entree?"

"The first was stuffed tongue. Cécile had prepared it with spring onions, strips of bacon and tomatoes cooked in a sauce seasoned with thyme, cloves, bay leaves and a small amount of lime juice. Next was served what the guests thought were ordinary meat balls. Dr. Johnson shook his head in refusal. His wife took a chance. With the first bite she forgot her dignity and said, 'Bring back that plate! George, if you don't taste this I'll never forgive you!' "

Lorena's enthusiasm was a weapon of conquest. "Next time," she said, "I'll bring my book and copy your recipes."

"If you do, I'll tell you how to make the meat balls" was the
rejoinder. "I will show you exactly how to cut the fillet, pound
it in the mortar and mix in the spices and the white of an egg.
I'll show you just how long to fry it in deep oil, and I'll even
serve it with rice and mushrooms, cashew nuts and shrimp!"

I didn't have a chance. Lorena was asking about the dessert.

"Ah, yes!" Reser recalled. "Pineapple sherbet in a hollowed-
out pineapple served on a design of pineapple leaves. Doctor
Newman asked Cécile how she got the idea for these things.
She said, 'I just thought it ought to be good like that!' That's
what I mean by inspiration. I tell you, *we* Haitians enjoy living.
You came down here to find out about Voodoo——"

"Right!" I cut in.

"You could do Haiti a greater service by telling Americans
that Haiti has been made the victim of much misrepresentation."

"What do you mean?" I asked.

"Tourists have been told a lot of nonsense about Haiti. They
have been warned not to eat meat down here. Why, meat is
washed in lime juice and cleaned more thoroughly than it is in
the States. They are cautioned not to eat green vegetables.
Ridiculous! They are told it is dangerous to go into the hills
alone. Why doesn't someone tell them that major crimes down
here are practically unknown. Sex crimes are rarely heard of.
There is no organized crime in Haiti. People are told a hundred
things about Haiti that are false, and these things ought to be
corrected."

"But you are right," I had to say. "We came down to learn
about Voodoo."

He disregarded my remark. "André," he called, and the boy
came running. Reser gave him his orders. Then, turning to us,
he said, "We are having coffee with sirup. You want to try it?"

"Merci," said Lorena. *"Café e dous."*

"Ai-yai-yai," exclaimed Reser happily, "that's the best thing you can do. Learn Creole."

"Oh," said Lorena, with thoughtful timing, "I know a very important Creole phrase."

"You do?" Reser's voice was skeptical. "Let's have it."

"Quitte um tiré portré ou?" She turned on the brightest light when she said that.

And Reser replied pleasantly, "To make it really effective say, *'Quitte um tiré portré ou, no?' No* is like adding 'Oh, please' or 'Come on.' Be sure you get the facial expression that goes with it." He demonstrated. "In Creole half of the conversation is voice, the other half, soul."

Lorena felt the stage perfectly set. "And," she asked, "if I should say to you, *'Quitte um tiré portré ou, no?'* what would you say, *M'sieur Docteur?"*

"Why," he replied, "I would say, *'Ou met tiré portré pa mué, ca pas fém ahien, mais ler moune yo pas vlé, quitte camera dého.'"*

"Which means?"

"'My picture you may take since I have no objections, but when you are with those who have objections, keep your camera away.' Ah, here is André with the coffee."

"André," said Lorena, *"quitte um tiré portré ou, no?"*

The boy was as astonished at the request as he was at hearing this foreigner's attempt at Creole. He looked to Reser for help, then took it upon himself to reply with a vigorous, *"No, no!"* and a shake of his head.

To put him at ease Reser spontaneously spun a Creole yarn, evidently something bearing upon the situation, for he soon had

André lost in musical laughter. With dramatic gestures and descriptive facial expression, Reser played upon the language as on an instrument. The close comradeship that existed between this strange white man and this native son of Haiti was again demonstrated. There were strong links of affection here, and when the story was over André ran out with happy, dancing steps.

"What magic do you work on these fellows?" I asked.

"That was just a story" was the casual reply. "A folk tale. These boys know the stories as well as I."

"But André acted as if he were hearing this one for the first time."

"It's the telling of it," Reser boasted with a laugh. "These stories must be word perfect and dramatized just right."

"You must have quite a repertory to find one to fit every occasion," Lorena observed.

"I know hundreds of them," Reser said. "Years ago, when I lived in north Haiti, the landlord had five children. Evenings the family would get together for story-telling time. That is where I learned the folk tales along with my Creole. If the narrator made a mistake, someone would correct him—'No, it goes this way. This is the way it must be.' It had to be perfect, like the Catholic Mass or the Voodoo ritual. I used to tell those stories to my two children, and now, even though they are back in the States, they tell them to theirs."

I questioned him on Voodoo ritual, to which he had referred.

He appeared not to hear. "I'll tell you a story," he said thoughtfully. "My son was a tail gunner during the war. He was wounded in action in the South Pacific. It was rumored that he had been killed. I went to a prominent *houngan*, a

Voodoo priest, living in the hills, and asked if he would call up a certain *loa,* a deity or saint, and get the facts. The *loa* said, 'This happened a long distance from here. Come back tomorrow and I will tell you.' When I returned he gave me this report: 'The boy is not dead. He was shot twice. Once in the hip. Once in the upper right side.' Which is where my son was wounded."

"And that is Voodoo?" I prodded.

"That," said Reser deliberately, "is the weight of proof of the existence of an extrasensory force and a demonstration that certain men can use that force."

"How else do they use it?"

Reser reflected a moment. His voice was serious. "Once," he recalled, "in the south of Haiti, a community had been troubled by the unwelcome visitation of an evil *loa,* a Petro *loa,* whom they referred to as Marinette. Any time a goat or a pig would disappear or a child would die or a house would burn or there would be an unusual run of bad luck, the people would say, 'Ah, that's Marinette.' So it was decided to hold a service to bind the *loa* for seventeen years. I knew that walking in fire and dancing in fire would be an important part of the service, so I planned to attend."

"What was the name of the community?" I asked and began making mental notes.

"It was in the Morne La Hotte region."

"Did you know any of the people?"

"I was living there," he said. "I knew them well. Very close to me lived a family in which was a girl of sixteen who was to be one of the main participants in the ceremony."

"What was her name?"

"Apela." He sipped his coffee as if unwilling to say more.

Lorena urged, "Please go on."

"I spent the entire afternoon and evening with the family," he continued. "I watched this girl to see if there was any preparation of her feet for the fire ordeal. There was none. I went with her and the family to a small plateau at the side of a ravine where the service was to be held. I never let Apela out of my sight. There was a pile of logs heaped up and a hole had been dug and filled with pitch pine. Then a pyramid of logs was built up and the truncated top was filled with shorter pieces of wood. Gallons of kerosene were poured on this, and then the fire was set. Soon the chanting and the drums mingled with the crackling flames. Men kept shoving the burning logs into the center as the dancing started. The sound of the *vaccines,* large bamboo flutes, the excited voices of the worshipers and the red glow of the fire built up an intense emotion. Nine members of the group became possessed. Apela was one of them."

"Possessed?" Lorena asked.

"Overpowered by a *loa,*" he explained. "Actually becoming the vehicle through which the *loa* is revealed. Then came the psychological moment. You can't tell how or why it comes. You can't predict when it will come. It is the moment of spiritual crisis. The possessed becomes a changed personality. Even though I knew that this was to happen, it struck me with an impact beyond my expectation. I saw Apela step into the fire. I watched her take seven slow, shuffling steps. I studied her face for signs of pain. There were none. The glow of the fire surrounded her with an aura. The others who were possessed had also stepped in. They, too, registered no pain, no fright, no reaction. They came out of the flames to make a circle around the fire and then went back for seven more steps. I could see the live coals topple over their feet. Their feet sank into the fiery embers. They walked back and forth until the coals were stamped out black."

"Could it have been——" I began.

He caught my thought. "Hypnotism? No! I know what I saw! I was at Apela's side when she stepped out after what seemed like an eternity in the fire. She and the others were offered food. She refused. A diviner took a whip and struck her across her back. There was no reaction, no sense of pain, no response. Finally she consented to eat. But it was not Apela who ate. It was Marinette. The food was offered to the *loa* through Apela and the acceptance of it was tantamount to a promise from Marinette to go away for seventeen years."

"Did you examine her feet after she came out?" I asked.

"Carefully. Closely. There was no evidence of blistering or burning. Her feet were absolutely normal in every respect. I asked her whether she remembered anything about walking through the fire. '*I* didn't walk through the fire,' she said. She was right. It was not Apela. It was the *loa*."

"And you believe this?" Lorena ventured.

Reser answered almost to himself. "When a man can intellectually accept what he feels in his heart, he has opened a door of faith that is not easily closed."

"I can see that you have made the intellectual hurdle," I said.

"Quite so." His tone was even and severe. "I have been forced to admit that there is an area in which the so-called primitive mind is more advanced than your so-called intellectuals. A *bocor,* a leaf doctor, knows more about herbs than your educated pharmacist. A diviner knows more about the function of good and evil spirits than your seminary-trained preacher. A Voodoo priest knows more about the source of creative power than does your theologian. And the peasant in his mountain shack lives closer to God than the society-spoiled city dweller." He suspected that we were skeptical at this pronouncement, and he dismissed the feeling with a wave of his hand. "Oh, well," he concluded, "someone once said that my spirit came from Africa."

I looked at him. The tropical sun, blazing in through the open door, made him half light and half shadow, a mysterious figure in a mysterious setting. His blue eyes penetrated into my thoughts.

"Every man," he said profoundly, "eventually finds a reason for his existence. When he finds it he realizes that the events of the past fall into a definite pattern. He knows then that there has been a design behind everything that has happened to him. This realization is life's greatest moment."

A shadow crossed the door. Reser called out in Creole and Diogène came in. Obeying a low word of instruction, the young man went to the other room and returned carrying against his body a large Voodoo drum. He gave it to Reser, who tested the taut drumhead and then put the instrument between his knees. Diogène watched with dreamy interest, and, when Reser began tapping out a rhythm, his body seemed to vibrate with the sound.

I glanced at Lorena and knew what she was thinking. Oh, for a camera! Reser the American became Reser the Haitian. The spirit from Africa took over. His face showed an inner ecstasy, his shoulders kept time to the one, two, *three,* one, two, *three* tapped out effortlessly, enchantedly with hypnotic appeal. It was the sound of the lonely drum, the voice beyond the hills saying, "Come to *me,* come to *me!*"

The simple beats, two unaccented and one accented, wove their spell. It was unnatural that the tap of human fingers could create such a fantasy so quickly, so unmistakably primitive, so frighteningly a part of the rhythm one felt in life. I closed my eyes to capture the sensation, to hold it and remember it. I tried to fix it in my mind, to analyze it, confident that I would re- member it always: the basic rhythm of the Congo. Then, in a moment, it changed to a more rapidly syncopated beat, driving out everything I thought I had learned.

I opened my eyes. Diogène and André stood in the room, their bodies moving almost imperceptibly, their eyes beaming, their faces beatific. Reser swayed with the sound of the drum- ming, a sound that grew in an exotic cadence. Louder and more sharply the staccato throb spun its magic. The primi- tive instrument gave forth a variety of tones on different keys, low and booming, then higher and more piercing. And as I watched the white man's flying hands and listened to the deep- ening Voodoo spell, I wondered whether Cicéron had suddenly entered the human form of this incredible American who claimed he had found life's greatest good and who believed that everything in the past had been but a preparation for his Haitian sojourn.

Lorena leaned over the table, chin in hands. I started writing down Voodoo drumbeats. Reser glanced at me, noticed what I was doing and brought his hands down on the drumhead in a sudden resounding beat.

"That," he exclaimed triumphantly, "is Nago! Write it by all means if you can. Nago, from Dahomey, Africa."

I had put the rhythm down: 1 2 3 4 **5**, 1 2 3 4 **5**, 1 2 **345**, 1 2 **3** 4 5 6, 1 2 **3** 4 5 6, 1 2 **3** 4 5 6, 1 2 **3** 4 5 6 7 8 **9**.

Would I ever forget it? Would it ever leave me? It was my introduction to the Haiti that lurked behind the hills and the people.

For an enchanted hour we absorbed Voodoo drumbeats as Reser transformed the cottage room into the African Congo. He always came back to that, the Congo rhythm: 1 2 **3**, 1 2 **3**, 1 2 **3**—come to *me,* come to *me,* come to *me!* The more complicated beats were explained to, but hardly understood by, Lorena and me: the *Jan Valo,* stately and austere, *Petro,* threatening and inciting passion, *Rara,* gay and exotic. It was Congo that never ceased to say, "Come to *me!*" It was Congo that was pounded into my mind, never to be forgotten. Reser explained that it could be heard throughout Haiti and all over Africa. Though every African tribe had its own special rhythm, Congo ran through them all like the river that gave it its name. He demonstrated how Congo formed the basis of jazz, was rudimental in our square dances, and he illustrated how, without modification, it was the rhythm of such songs as "Golden Slippers," "Turkey in the Straw," and "Dance to the Light of the Moon." He played these, humming the melody, and ending each number with a triumphant cry, "Pure Congo!"

He showed us the tremendous effect of the *fent,* how a drummer makes believe he is going to strike and then "holds up" until a psychological moment. We began to understand how a Voodoo drummer works on his dancers. Reser almost convinced us that through the power and unbelievable latitude of the drum a *loa* could be invoked and possession could be induced.

"And yet—" he sighed—"you have heard nothing in my playing. Nothing at all. Perhaps a small one third of what you should hear. For there are three drums at the services: one like this, the *maman* drum, then the *seconde,* and a still smaller one, the *cata* or *boula. Houn* is the spirit of the drum. That is why the drums are also named the *hounto, hountoti* and *hounlaki.* When a person salutes the battery of drums he always salutes the little one first."

"I'll remember that," said Lorena. "When do we start? When do we go to a service?"

Reser took two knives from the table. *"Ai-yai-yai!"* he said to Diogène and André. Then turning to us: "I almost forgot. There are not only the drums, there is also the *ogan,* two pieces of steel which are struck together like this."

Demonstrating with the knives, he showed us that the spirit of the drums could be captured and incited by the *ogantier* in a variety of startling sounds.

"Lorena had a good question, Doctor Reser," I said. "When do we start?"

He leaned back in his chair and looked at us indulgently. As if in response to a thought, André brought him a pipe and tobacco. Reser thanked him.

"If and when we go," he said, smiling, "always remember that the Haitian peasant never lets a chance go by to steal from heaven a moment of joy." Stuffing his pipe, he repeated this to his Haitian friends in Creole. André struck a match and handed it to him.

"The moment of realization!" Reser said contentedly. "For more than half my life I kept looking for an intangible something. It was the eternal background for all my thoughts. When I was a Utah Mormon I thought I might find it in that faith.

I looked for it in Protestantism, and for years I also searched for it in Catholicism. When I studied it was to gain knowledge to help me find it. When I traveled it was in the hope that somewhere it might be discovered. I sailed the seas and visited many countries. Where could it be? Just what was this something I was seeking?"

He smoked in silence. "Some things cannot be put into words," he mused. "The deepest things are feelings—sensations. I only know that when I first set foot on Haitian soil I knew that I had found it. The pearl of great price. When I breathed the air of Haiti something whispered to me, 'You are home.' When I went to my first Voodoo service I had only one desire. I asked God to help me shake off all sophistication and begged heaven to give me the trusting soul of a peasant."

He ended this testimonial by getting up resolutely and taking the drum into the other room.

Lorena looked at me as if to ask, Is all of this getting us anywhere? Will we ever get him to commit himself?

I said aloud, "All of this certainly gives a person a different slant on Voodoo."

From the other room came a triumphant "Aha! And you said you had no preconceived ideas!"

Somewhat daunted at the acute hearing of the man, I called back, "Well, *most* people think of Voodoo only in terms of cannibalism and witchcraft, snake worship and black magic. . . ."

I heard him guffaw loudly.

Lorena whispered to me, "I should think that if he really felt this way about Voodoo he'd want to help us find out the truth about it."

"Yes," I whispered back, "in picture and in story."

Reser came back into the room. In his hands he held a vial filled with small white pills. In a perfunctory manner he set the bottle before us on the table.

"If we are going together," he said, "I wish you would each take three of these pills."

Lorena reached for the bottle.

"What are they?" I asked.

Lorena unscrewed the cap.

"Take three," Reser ordered. "And take them regularly. You won't have to worry about malaria."

I watched Lorena tap three of the white pellets into the palm of her hand. She tossed them into her mouth and washed them down with coconut milk. I looked at her to see what would happen! Nothing happened. She handed the bottle to me.

"I'll take them later," I promised.

"Take the bottle with you," said our host. "Three a week is the right dosage."

"Later," I said.

Lorena watched as I dropped the bottle into my pocket. She knew, even better than I, my aversion to pills of any kind and probably already suspected that I would never take them.

4.

WE STAYED at the Chez Pauline until mid-afternoon. By that time we had elicited a promise from Reser that he would take us to a Voodoo ceremony in the near future. He had opened these tantalizing doors for outsiders on at least two previous occasions: once for Katherine Dunham and once

for Lily Pons and Andre Kostelanetz. He had also befriended
novelist Zora Neale Hurston and had provided Ivan T. Sander-
son with valuable inclusions for *Caribbean Treasure*.

He would not say just when a service would be held but explained that the Voodoo liturgical calendar followed closely
the holy days of the Christian year. Not that Voodoo and Christianity were on friendly terms so far as institutionalized religion
was concerned, but the Haitian peasant's instinctive urge to
worship had never recognized a distinction between "true" and
"pagan" practices in the search for God.

When the first bewildered African was dragged from his
slave ship and heard for the first time the stories of saints and
miracles he said, "This is nothing new. We have our own
deities, and they, too, have done great things. We have our
magic and our mysteries. The only difference between your
God and ours is that yours permits you to be masters over men,
and ours asks us to let all men be free." He added the new
saints and Jesus to his favorite *loa* and adapted his primitive fes-
tivals to the Christian observances. Days important to the Catholic Church were now also noteworthy in the *hounfort,* the
Voodoo chapel. Since we were in Haiti during the Advent season, we would not have long to wait for a Voodoo debut.

With this assurance we prepared to return to our hotel. Reser
suggested that the easiest way back to Port-au-Prince would be
to take a *camion,* an open bus with straight wooden seats, which
we could catch on Bizoton Road. He offered to escort us to a
bus stop by means of a trail which only the natives used.

To our surprise this secret path skirted the grounds of the estate and was reached by a short walk from Reser's home. The
moment we entered it I knew that Lorena was composing a men-

tal map so that she could surely find it again. It was a lane that knew nothing about the modern world and disdained infringing on the hedged-in property which we had just left. This sequestered footpath had been here long before the island ever heard of General Leclerc.

The people walking here were pilgrims in a timeless procession. They emerged from the wooded settings into the softly diffused light to tell the story of the Haiti that had won its liberty against tremendous odds. English corsairs and French and Spanish invaders had not robbed them of their right to walk freely from their mountain homes to the market places. This was their thoroughfare, where the ground was moist and cool beneath their bare feet, where their burdens were lightened by the peace that nature shed upon them and where liberating shade and silence brought sudden relaxation.

I paused instinctively to view this passing parade, wondering whether Reser was conscious of the rhythmic pad of the trotting feet, whether he saw the incongruity in the happily chatting women stalwartly bearing the heavy burdens on their heads, carrying limp, jogging babies on their backs and unconcernedly dangling strings of chickens over their shoulders. I wondered whether he felt, as I did, that this procession of peasant pilgrims, this Haiti, wanted nothing more than to be left alone, left to itself, left to live its life without being tracked down and inquisitively explored.

My questions were answered immediately. Reser was one of the people. He belonged in this fellowship. He was wanted. *"Bonjour, Docteur!"* was the spontaneous greeting. "Hi, Doc!" and "Ah, *M'sieur Docteur!"* were friendly salutations that included us as well. Reser the Haitian emerged naturally to play his part, and the contagion of his spirit drew us into the scene as welcome extras in an expanding cast.

He paused frequently to inquire about some member of a family or to relate a brief story or proverb. His impulsive *"Ai-yai-yai!"* was a cry of recognition as he caught sight of an old friend, and his enthusiasm was shared with us. He could not take us to Bizoton Road without first showing us the watering fountain where the women dipped up the cool water with calabashes and where the market people rested in the tranquil shade. The scene brought moans from Lorena wishing for her camera.

"Is it always like this?" she asked. "Are there always such interesting people here and burros standing, and women squatting on their skirts as if they were sitting in hammocks? Is the light always this mellow and the shadows so perfect?"

"Always!" was the proud response. "A perfect setting for a Haitian pastorale."

"Don't you ever come here to sketch?" she implored.

"Why should I come here?" Reser argued lightly. "I have all of this in my mind. I know these people. I know how they look and how they think. I have sketched them, but not for exploitation. Painting opened up a whole new world to me. It made me realize that I had been going through life half blind. I photograph scenes with my mind, and no one can object to that. When I first began doing that I said to myself, If you can absorb the minutest details with your vision, you can also do it with the rest of your senses. You have never really used to their fullest degree sound, hearing, taste and touch. That meant a new and deeper interpretation of music, language, food, physical objects. Life became a series of sense impressions. It was a revolutionary discovery. But why should you be so anxious about the picture possibilities here? Everywhere you look in Haiti you see a picture."

Lorena was reluctant to be consoled with a phrase. The deep shade cast by the shiny dark-green leaves of the famous mapou tree gave a steady and dramatic lighting effect. The mountain forming the western background was crowned with flamboyants, majestic with their huge central trunks and still bearing clusters of long brown pods. A fence, red-covered with bougainvillea vines, nearly concealed the banana grove and provided a vast perspective as it led off into the distance.

Reser escorted us down the trail in the direction of Bizoton Road, describing the trees and shrubs with as much familiarity as if he had planted them.

"That's a Caladium, an aroid," he explained. "There's a cainito, the star apple. Here are breadfruit trees and mangoes."

He led us off to the left into a narrower lane which wound through a peasant village. No one who came to Pauline's paradise through the front way or sat in the exclusive surroundings of the estate would ever have dreamed that here, within a few minutes' walk, was this other world.

The homes were mud-plastered, with palm-thatched roofs. Through open doorways we caught sight of the inevitable sleeping mats. Reser described in minute detail how these were made by stripping off layer after layer of a banana plant, drying them in the sun, then rolling up the dried strips into tight, springy rolls and tying them together.

He took us into the hut of a friend to show us a *dessoir*. This was a kind of whatnot made of mahogany and provided with shelves for holding glasses, cups and dinnerware. We were also shown the *cruche,* a huge crock of porous red clay that kept the drinking water cold in the hottest weather. And there was the *garde mange,* a screened mahogany cupboard where food, cooked and uncooked, could be kept out of the way of insects. A homemade table and chairs, a mirror and some lithographs of the saints completed the tidy interior. Anyone looking for poverty could find it, but the spice-laden air was a common treasure shared by all. Bowers of palm fronds and poinsettias showered beauty around many a humble home.

We passed a makeshift brush canopy propped up on stilts. Under it were two crude backless benches. Reser called this shelter a *tonnelle,* a place where Voodoo services are held. Farther on in an unkempt yard a small wooden cross was stuck into the ground. On it dangled a battered black hat with a pair of castoff spectacles fixed to the brim. Around this was a small pile of stones. It looked like a comical marker over a deserted grave, but Reser said seriously, "Guedé, an important *loa.* Guedé Nibo, guardian of the dead."

He bowed in solemn greeting to the cross and hat. He led us on, singing half aloud a song to Guedé:

> *Guedé ti moun,*
> *Yo wé,*
> *Relé yo,*
> *Guedé Nibo loa.*

I asked him to translate it, and he said, "Guedé child, they will see. Call them. Guedé Nibo is my *loa.*"

"Have *you* ever seen Guedé?" I asked.

"Have I seen Guedé?" he echoed. *"Ai-yai-yai!* Many a time! Guedé is one of the most interesting of all the *loa.* He is always entertaining. And remarkably psychic. He bathes his face and washes his wide-open eyes in pimento peppers hotter than tabasco sauce, yet there are no harmful effects."

"How can you see a *loa?*" Lorena wanted to know. *"Loa* are spirits."

"They are seen during possession. When a *loa* possesses a person he sees the *loa.* Guedé dresses in black and often lavender. He smokes a big cigar. He sings risqué songs and swings a hula hip that a Hawaiian would envy. Often he will say, 'Laugh with me, but don't try to make a fool of me! Laugh with me, but don't laugh at me! Sweep and sprinkle, mow it and leave it, no wrong side, no right side, foam on the avalanche. Master of the cemetery . . . *ago . . . agoci . . . agola!'* "

He was carried away by thoughts of Guedé and walked along as though his heart were free.

Lean dogs foraged hopefully for food in the barren yards, and hungry-looking children sucked at stubs of sugar cane. Families sat in their swept-out clearing or worked, weaving sisal or carving pieces of mahogany.

"Bonjour, Docteur Reser!"

"Komma ou ye, Doc!" ("How are you, Doc?")

"Hi, Doc!"

From the smallest naked child to the eldest peasant, the recognition was complete. Reser was a fellow citizen. The only difference between him and the people was the color of his skin, and that distinction, apparently, had long been forgotten.

We were passing a dull-red clay-coated *caille* when we heard an excited cry, "Doc! Doc Reser!"

A thin-faced Haitian came running from the yard. He stopped short, as if suddenly realizing that Reser was not alone, hesitated a moment, then shouted, "Doc! *Loa a vini!"*

Reser said, *"Nan tete qui moune?"*

"Ou pas con moune na!" answered the man.

"What is he saying?" I asked.

"He says, 'The *loa* has just come!' I asked him, 'In whose head?' He said, 'You don't know the person.' We must go and see."

Now we heard the sound of the *ogan,* the pieces of steel banged together. Rhythmic clangor settled into a stinging, high-pitched beat. A weird chant sung by a woman rose over it.

"Aha, aha!" Reser exclaimed, pausing to listen. "It's an Ibo song. Sure enough, it is Ibo *lélé!"*

We followed closely behind him, Lorena clamoring for an explanation.

"An Ibo *loa* is favoring someone with a visitation" was the reply. "Ibo *loa* are of African origin. They are very helpful but demand strict fulfillment of all obligations. We are very lucky to be here just now. I have attended only four Ibo services in all my years in Haiti."

"Is this actually a Voodoo service?" I asked.

"It is a Voodoo manifestation, a case of sudden possession," Reser said.

The Haitian had gone quickly to the rear of the house and was beckoning for *M'sieur Docteur* to come. In a flurry of Creole, Reser put him at ease, and the man smiled broadly. We were now at the back entrance where a door hung on a single hinge. The Haitian stood aside, giving Reser the honor of entering first.

"Come along," Reser invited, and we followed him in.

The floor of the house was the tamped-down earth. The dark-ocher walls were adobe. A shaft of sunlight, streaming through a narrow window, was the only bright touch in these cavernous surroundings, and it led like a luminous carpet to the room where the chanting and the *ogan* were building their spell.

Reser entered the adjoining room through the low door; Lorena and I were close behind him. We almost stumbled over a young man who sat cross-legged in a shadowy corner at our left. He was the *ogantier,* banging together two discarded automobile valves. This incongruity was impressive! Voodoo, old as the Congo, had at least this one contemporary touch. The *ogantier* saw nothing strange in this. He was happily entranced. His eyes roved over us ecstatically. He was an automaton, recording with elegant abandon the impulses of a hidden spring of faith.

In the center of the small room was the chanting woman. She was middle-aged and dressed in white, pirouetting and swaying in a state of possession. From beneath her quivering eyelids she looked into space. There was the evidence of inner tranquillity about her despite the seizures that controlled her body. This was not a case of hysteria. She had evidently become the willing intermediary for an invading presence striving to make itself known.

At the end of the room a young girl sat before a simple altar in an attitude of prayer. The altar was about two feet high. On it were earthen bottles, jars, plates, calabash bowls, a vase of flowers, a crucifix, a cologne bottle and several glasses in which small wicks were burning. On the wall behind the altar were colored lithographs of Catholic saints.

It was Reser who held our attention. He walked into this situation with priestly authority. As he looked at the possessed woman he said half aloud, "The color of Ibo is red." This seemed to cause him momentary concern, for she was, as we

had noticed, in white. However, he satisfied himself that the
possession was Ibo, for on the floor was a corn-flour drawing of
a *canari* or water jar, the *loa's* symbol.

Reser studied this design, called a *veve,* for a moment. He
made several mystical signs, much like the sign of the cross, and
moved toward the altar. The girl greeted him. He questioned
her for a moment. Then he selected an urn from the altar,
lifted it up, murmured a fervent Creole prayer and proceeded
to sprinkle a libation in the four corners of the room.

The possessed woman chanted happily. Apparently the *loa*
was pleased. The proper ceremony was being enacted. Reser
addressed the *loa: "Soi Ibo soi, Ibo soiment!"* The prescribed
litany was being recited. The *ogantier* tapped the automobile
valves with an icy, biting sound. The girl at the altar prayed
solemnly. *M'sieur Docteur* was a worthy priest for this household visitation and filled the room with an expression of joy.
He danced and sang an Ibo song:

> *Iamon san y san é!*
> *Con ca dansé Ibo!*
> *Con ca dansé Ibo!*
> *Ibo lelé, Ibo lelé!*
> *Pilé pie'm pas mandé pardon,*
> *Pilé pie'm pas mandé pardon,*
> *Ca pardon fé pou misé?*

> Like that they dance Ibo!
> Like that they dance Ibo!
> Ibo sing, Ibo sing!
> Step on my foot, don't ask pardon,
> Step on my foot, don't ask pardon,
> What does pardon do for me?

Haitians began filling the doorway behind us, closing us in, casting the room into near darkness. I glanced at those who had come to watch and saw in their expressions their trusting faith made manifest. They beheld, in the woman in possession, proof of the existence of the *loa* and positive evidence that communication between mortals and immortals was still a Voodoo function.

Reser stood before the *ogantier,* giving approval to the hypnotic Ibo beat. Again he addressed the *loa. "Soi Ibo soi!"* From the altar he took a *canari* which resembled the corn-flour drawing on the floor. He took two short palm fronds and improvised drumsticks, then got down on his knees and beat out the Ibo rhythm on the mouth of the jar. The loud, resonant tone throbbed through the room.

As I watched the gyrating figure of the possessed woman and heard the "drum" and the *ogan* I realized how closely this demonstration in a lowly Haitian home paralleled a phenomenon I had frequently witnessed among the extreme holiness people in America. There, under the power of what was called the "baptism of the Spirit," the recipient also showed the unmistakable signs of possession and change in personality. In both instances there was the same inspired dancing, the same rolling of the eyes and chanting under the influence of an empowering force. In Christianity it was the "Spirit." In Voodoo it was the *loa.*

And here was Stanley Reser, this multipersonality, blending a religious tradition of north and south, weaving together white and black, fusing in his mysterious nature two cultures, two races, two ideological systems and, for all I knew, two gods.

The question, What is Voodoo? was becoming more complex. The question, Who and what is Stanley Reser? seemed even more insolvable.

Lorena touched my arm. She, too, was held by the dramatic sight of this indomitable white man as he controlled by his words and actions the sway and temper of the woman in possession. All eyes were fixed on him. He picked up the *canari* and carried it to a spot near the corn-flour design. The magnetic lines of power were the *loa's*, but the governing agency, the guidance for the phenomenon flowed from Reser. Now he dropped the jar deliberately. It broke open, and the breaking was accompanied by an electrical reaction on the part of the possessed woman. She suddenly calmed. Her features changed. She was like one released from a hypnotic spell. She gazed around with seeing eyes. Reser stood in an attitude of great reverence, his head lowered as if bowing to the will of some conquering force.

Lorena looked at me questioningly. Her glance was a reflection of my thought. She, too, was thinking, Is it possible that this man is himself a Voodoo priest?

Chapter 2

I HAD TOLD RESER THAT I HAD NO preconceived ideas about Voodoo, but sometimes I wondered. Two books had long stood side by side on the family shelf: Spenser St. John's *Hayti* and Seabrook's *The Magic Island*.

The first took as its theme the lament of Louis Napoleon: "Hayti! Hayti! Land of the barbarians!" Its author contended that if Napoleon had known the particulars relating to "Vaudoux worship" he would have expressed himself more violently. St. John claimed that the Voodooists were gangs of cannibals who stole water from Pauline's swimming pool and used it in cooking the flesh of their human sacrifices. He reported that there was not a single district in Haiti where cannibalism did not exist just prior to the turn of the present century and predicted for the Black Republic a period of "rapid decadence" into complete primitivism.

Seabrook picked up from there. He gave the impression that Voodoo was composed mainly of sex and superstition. I never forgot his "goat-cry girl-cry" in which a "blood-maddened, sex-maddened, god-maddened" people paid their respects to a "hermaphroditic deity."

Later I ran across Richard Loederer's *Voodoo Fire in Haiti*.

He accused Voodoo of hanging like a pall over the land and striking terror into the lives of the people. He denounced the *papaloi* and the *mamaloi*—terms which, according to Reser, were never heard in Haiti—for keeping the natives in dread and fear. Loederer claimed he attended a Voodoo service and described it as "pure sexuality."

Faustin Wirkus, in his *The White King of La Gonave,* gave me a picture of Voodoo as centering around a black pope and black queens and flourishing in a series of sexual orgies. After spying upon the clandestine worship he interpreted Voodoo liturgy against the background of his own "highly civilized" concepts and tried to stamp it out with gunshot and the sword. There stuck in my mind a series of wild scenes of passion which he witnessed from the cover of darkness and criticized from behind the protection of his armed men.

Almost every book and every newspaper story had sensationalized Voodoo. Most accounts which I had heard before coming to Haiti had labeled it a snake pit of superstition, had talked about zombis, who were the "living dead," and about *wangas* (curse charms) and fetishes used to put the hex on people and work out their witchery of evil and death.

Voodoo had also crept into my vocabulary by way of Vachel Lindsay and into my blood through the spell of his "Congo." Through him I first heard the screaming of the fife and the scraping of bare feet around the sacred fires. With him I had felt the throb of hidden drums, the drone of tom-toms, the wailing of fanatical black worshipers, and in those days the mumbo jumbo of the god of the Congo had voodooed me.

Something else had happened. Before Lorena and I boarded the plane at Camagüey, Cuba, I had picked up some mail.

Among the letters was a warning from a friend, Paul Ramsey, whose premonitions of things to come had frequently proved startlingly correct. Ramsey had written me in sprawling black, "Don't go to Haiti! Voodoo is of the devil. It's snake worship and black magic. Your excursions into obscure religions in America are one thing. Your trip into Voodoo is something else. Don't go to Haiti!"

I thought of these things on the evening scheduled for a meeting with Stanley Reser. Lorena and I were going to our first Voodoo service with a man whom we had known only three days. I had known Vachel Lindsay and my letter-writing friend all my life. Who was right? But since I had always depended on intuition as the touchstone in my research, I could only follow the hunch that Reser was trustworthy and sincere.

Lorena had agreed. Realizing that this fabulous figure was our only source of admittance into Voodoo's inner shrine, she had promised to leave her cameras at the hotel and conform to Reser's stipulation that "pictures are out."

I suspected that she was assenting so readily only because she had enjoyed a good harvest of interesting shots that afternoon in the hills around Kenscoff. A cab had taken her to the end of the road at two o'clock, and she had walked toward Furcy. She worked until after five asking, *"Quitte um tiré portré ou, no?"* Surprisingly enough, she had succeeded every once in a while in getting dubious or reluctant co-operation, but she was not above sniping from behind a tree or the tall grass.

She did get one wonderful shot legitimately. A peasant girl was climbing a mountain trail bearing on her head a large tin container nearly filled with water. The container had a small puncture in one corner, and the water was leaking out as from a drippy faucet. With great dexterity the girl was balancing on her left shoulder a small tin can to catch the precious drops.

As soon as Lorena got back to the hotel I locked her in the wardrobe closet, tacked up the blankets and awaited "developments." The negatives looked perfect. She was beginning to build up a Haitian documentary, but it was Voodoo she was after.

2.

RESER came jauntily up the walk as if assuring the world that Haiti held a youthful elixir.

"Man-o-man!" he exclaimed with a hearty laugh. "I'm still chuckling over what just happened. I met a woman from Carrefour who had a little girl toddling at her side. I asked, 'What's the child's name?' 'Fatra,' the woman said. 'Fatra?' I laughed. 'That means trash! Why do you call her Fatra?' 'I have a good reason,' she said. 'If the devil comes along and asks her name and she says it is Fatra, he won't want her!' That's what makes Haiti so interesting. The unseen world is as real to these people as the physical world. They walk with the spirits as naturally as they walk with their friends."

"Shall we say they are unusually superstitious?"

"They aren't," he replied. "Every culture has its superstitions. Every country has its idiosyncracies. In America there is the superstition about walking under ladders. Here you won't catch a Haitian stepping over a rope on a tethered animal. Catholics wear the Agnus Dei. Here many children wear some-

thing similar to Job's-tears to ward off the evil eye. Some
Americans have a superstition about wearing a hat in the house.
A Haitian will always take his hat off crown down. He will
never win a case in court if he tips his hat any other way. You
believe in four-leaf clovers and horseshoes for good luck. In
many a Haitian home you will see an ear of corn, burned in
the fire until black. That spells good luck for them. Many
religions believe in blessing medals and charms. Voodoo has
its *paquets* or talismans containing flowers and spices which are
said to have therapeutic value. There are superstitions all over
the world having to do with words and phrases. A Haitian
won't tell stories until after sundown. Something will happen
to his mother if he does."

"Do these things all tie in with Voodoo?"

"Does your belief about black cats tie in with Christianity?
Almost every superstition can be traced back to religion. The
same is true of nearly every science. Alchemy was the forerun-
ner of chemistry. Astrology led to astronomy. Hypnotism gave
rise to psychiatry. Spiritism was responsible for theology. The
so-called superstitions about planting led to the science of agri-
culture. A Haitian still plants squashes and melons only during
the full of the moon. He has a particular phase of the moon
for all his planting. Herbs and magic are the parents of medicine. All this is Voodoo."

"What do you mean?"

"Voodoo is the oldest link in the chain between faith and
knowledge. Haitians believe, for example, that concoctions of
yellow flowers are good for jaundice. How did they get this
knowledge? First by faith. By a belief. Then they proved it.
Haitians generally beware of night air and protect themselves
from dew. Women after ironing will hesitate to go out into

the cool air. Negroes as a race have very little immunity against respiratory infections. But they are, apparently, immune to tropical diseases which would kill a white person, while a white man can go out in all sorts of weather. All this was first a matter of belief, then knowledge. Beets, they told me, are good for anemia. I asked why. They shrugged and said, 'We just know.' I once suffered from a serious colonic disturbance, and all the medical knowledge I had did me no good. An old woman living in the house went out into the hills one morning and brought back some cactus leaves. She prepared an infusion from the leaves of a plant called *swiss* and the cactus leaves. I drank it and was cured within a few hours."

"Was she a Voodooist?"

He dismissed the question with a wave of his hands. "Who is a Voodooist and who isn't?"

"How many of the natives are, would you say?"

"How many Americans are Christians?" was the retort. "Who knows? You can't identify religion only with its institutional expression."

"I suppose," I reasoned, "in times of need many people turn to Voodoo just as in the States many frequently turn to the Church."

"That's right. There once was a Haitian who had suffered with asthma for many years. Finally he went to a *bocor,* a leaf doctor, who prescribed *ouary* beans. These were roasted and pounded into a powder and taken in a glass of water. The asthmatic tried the prescribed dosage for four or five days and found that it had no effect. He doubled the dosage. A short time later his asthma was gone, but his body was covered with blisters, and he was terribly afflicted with conjunctivitis. He could hardly see. After a short time the blisters dried up, the skin peeled off and to his amazement all the dark pigment in his skin disappeared. He was pinkish-white like a young baby. He was now an albino. He was taken to the States and examined by physicians. I met the man afterward, and he had developed quite a color prejudice. In talking to me he always said, 'We white men.' All of this is Haiti—part of its faith and part of its knowledge. But Americans don't want this. They want zombis and snakes and *wangas*."

"Voodoo isn't zombis and snakes and *wangas?*"

He thought for a long moment before he replied. "Voodoo," he said stubbornly, "is Voodoo. There *is* black magic. There are *wangas* that have the power of death."

"And zombis?" I insisted.

I waited for his explanation about these "living dead," but he only said, "There are charlatans in Voodoo just as there are in every other religion. But there are also high-type *houngans* and *mambos* of the kind you will see tonight."

"Is there a way to test them?"

"Certainly. Good priests do good. Evil ones do evil."

I asked him how one got to be a Voodoo priest or priestess and he countered, "How does one get to be a spiritualistic medium? Or a musician? Or a minister? He has special aptitudes and qualifications. He has a 'call.' In Voodoo it is often the call of the *loa* who comes in a dream or during a state of possession. Sometimes a person has been serving as *la place* to a *houngan*. *La place* might be called an associate priest. Or he may have been a *hounsi*. The *hounsi* are much the same as acolytes. Just as acolytes in Catholicism often feel a call to become priests, so the *hounsi* or *la place* may feel called to study for the Voodoo priesthood."

"Is the Voodoo priesthood organized?"

"Mystically it is, but not in any hierarchical sense."

"The priests are trained?"

"By the master-disciple method. There is a long period of detailed instruction followed by ceremonies of initiation and induction. The candidate must be word-perfect in the ritual, prayers and hymns. Contrary to most ministerial requirements, the Voodoo priest is expected to have not only a knowledge of things but also a power over things. His training is not merely theoretical. It is not enough that he knows. He must be able also to perform."

"Not only faith, but works?"

"Exactly."

"What kind of works? What kind of power?"

"He must know the use of herbs and have the power of healing. But he must have a knowledge beyond that of the *bocor.* The *houngan* is an adept in the field of psychic treatment. He is psychiatrist, general practitioner and spiritual priest. He must have the ability to speak *langage,* the language of the *loa.* He must know how to communicate with the deities, how to invoke the forces of good and drive away the forces of evil. In short, the *houngan* lives close to the supernatural. He has *quatre yeux,* four eyes. This means that he is given sight beyond normal vision. He is clairvoyant. He sees what other men do not see. He hears what other men do not hear. If a priest has no supernormal powers, what right has he to the priesthood? If he cannot demonstrate psychically, away with him. If a priest is no nearer to God's secrets than a layman, he is no priest. That, it seems to me, is fair enough."

"Have you ever seen the initiatory ceremonies?"

"Have I!" he exclaimed. "I have seen many, my friend. They include periods of fasting and meditation that few people know anything about and would care even less to undertake. There is, for example, *kanzo*."

"*Kanzo?*"

"The baptism of fire," he mused.

"Symbolical?"

"If you are asking whether it has a symbolical meaning, yes. If you ask whether the initiate really exposes himself to the flames, the answer is also yes. He puts his hands into the fire and is not burned."

"On such things," I said, "I'll withhold judgment until I have seen them."

He shrugged off my remark with a proverb: " '*Faut al' la pou con la.*' "

"Which is to say?"

" 'You must go there to know there.' "

"I only meant to say," I answered, "that common sense tells me there are things *you* tell me about Voodoo that are hard to believe."

His reply was instant, as though he had heard this remark before. "I am in accord with the savant Flammarion. He said that 'common sense' is often just another term for general ignorance."

Since I had nothing to add to this, he was disinclined to say more. Voodoo with him was a certainty, and he wanted to make sure that I knew exactly where he stood. If I had any idea that he was a dilettante in this field or an outsider looking in, he wanted such opinions dispelled. We sat in silence while the *loa* beyond the hills gently touched the skies with their own crimson fires, and the purple shadows in the yard deepened.

Reser lighted a cigarette, held the burning match a moment

and said with meaningful reflection, *"Kanzo."* Then he tossed the match away.

Beyond the gateway the pageantry of Haiti passed by. The silhouetted basket carriers, the burros, the taxis with their honking horns staged their unceasing ballet. A shoeshine boy came up the walk tapping a soft rhythm on his bootblack box to attract attention. In the distance I could hear the plaintive and familiar "Gee-e-a-a-a-a-az" of the kerosene vendors.

A young girl, stove-black, dressed in rags, strolled up to us begging, "Gimme five cents, gimme five cents." This was obviously the only English she knew, and she was one who must have considered Reser a newcomer to Haiti along with me. He waited until she stood before us with pleading hands. Then with a change in voice and personality he said in his excellent Creole, "Look here, little girl! Don't embarrass me before strangers. I just told the man that Haitians are not beggars. Now you make a liar out of me. You must never ask money from foreigners. That will give them a bad impression of us. Remember that, my child!"

She looked at him as if she had seen a zombi and drew away. She walked backward with her eyes fixed on him until she reached the gate. Then she turned and ran.

3.

I WENT up to see what was keeping Lorena. She was washing the last batch of negatives under the coldwater tap in our room.

She hurried down and her *"Kouma ou ye, M'sieur* Reser?"

pleased him. She had worked on this phonetic version of How
are you? so successfully that he complimented her.

"Creole is very simple," he explained. "There are only some
two thousand basic words. No verb conjugations. You won't
even need to learn an alphabet. Once you catch on, Creole
speaks itself."

He always made everything appear easy, and we were usually
prepared to leave all arrangements to him. We did just that
when we got into a cab on the Champs de Mars. He sat with
the driver, carrying on his usual spirited conversation. I gathered he was giving directions about the route and inquiring
whether the road would be passable all the way. Roads in Haiti,
I was learning, usually were not.

We drove westward, and as darkness deepened and there
was no indication that our driver would turn on the lights,
Lorena said, *"Pouqui ca* ... that is ... *ou pa lumé* ... lights ...
lumé ye?"

The stolid driver turned halfway around only because she
was nudging him in the back.

Reser addressed him in Creole. "Madame wants to know
how you can see." Then he translated the reply. "He says,
'Battery is bad, but eyes are good.'"

Like other Port-au-Prince cabbies this one was always saving
the battery, apparently so there would be more power left for
honking the horn. Like every other driver of a *ligne* he complained that the cars were rented, that they cost twenty-five
gourdes (five dollars) a day and that no one could make
money at such a price. I told Reser to tell him about the driver
who took me to the post office that morning. In answer to my
inquiry about the fare, my driver had said, "For those who

know, it is ten cents, for those who don't know, it's twenty."

Finally our man turned on the lights. In the unsteady yellow glow we saw the people, the peasants, trudging through the cool of the night. Tomorrow and for a thousand tomorrows in Haiti they would be making their way to city markets in Port-au-Prince, Saint Marc, Cap-Haïtien, Mirebalais, to street markets in villages and towns, to roadside markets where settlements had sprung up along the way. These peasant pilgrims, who found their way instinctively through the narrow jungle trails by day or night, went sure-footedly and unerringly on the highways. Reser said they had a sharper night vision than the white man and a sixth sense that guided them here as elsewhere along the way of life.

Some of them rested with their loaded burros. A few of the women hovered over charcoal fires, squatting on their skirts in the characteristic way. But for the most part they walked, young and old together, silent and untiring, with the precarious baskets on their heads and burdens on their backs.

Reser gave a sudden order and we swerved into a deserted wagon road. This turnoff could not have been maneuvered without lights, however keen our driver's sight. Large stones seemed to have been put in the way deliberately, and the ruts were scraping-deep. After a hazardous half mile Reser decided we would walk, and he arranged with our somber cabby that he should meet us at this spot at two in the morning. It was now nearly ten.

The driver generously gave us the benefit of the dwindling lights, and, as we walked out of their dissolving yellow fringe, Reser led off across uneven ground. Lorena and I followed convinced that Doc Reser, too, had cat's eyes.

We trudged across bogs and wallows with the outline of the brooding mountains rising almost within reach. I chided Lorena for having left her pocket flashlight at the hotel. Now when we needed it, it was safely in her wardrobe darkroom. It is doubtful whether we would ever have tried to find this place without a guide. How would we have gone about it alone? I still felt confronted by the impassable barrier of language and the uncertainty as to just what awaited an intruder into the Voodoo realm, but I had a growing feeling of confidence in this man Reser.

As if sensing this, he called back to us, "Going to a service should be a happy time. Listen, and I'll teach you a little song."

It was in this setting, as we stumbled on through the dark, that we learned the few lines and the lilting melody of:

> *Jé innocent, jé innocent, bon a ye,*
> *Jé innocent, jé innocent, bon a ye.*
> *Nan point rien pleu fort passe Bon Dié,*
> *Jé innocent, jé innocent, bon a ye.*
>
> Innocent eyes, innocent eyes, good will see,
> Innocent eyes, innocent eyes, good will see.
> There is nothing stronger than God,
> Innocent eyes, innocent eyes, good will see.

Alerted suddenly by Reser's low "Oh-o, oh-o!" we felt rather than saw the people. We were startled by the quick nearness of a small group of men, but Reser greeted them familiarly. In the distance we caught sight of the flicker of candles, the shadowy contour of a thatch-roofed pavilion and the outline of moving figures. The men surrounded Reser and led us forward.

We were about twenty feet from the pavilion when Reser stopped. Our escorts melted into the shadows. From the building emerged a tall, slender Haitian woman wearing a white turban and attired in a simple white dress. She was flanked by several girls bearing candles. Stopping a short distance from Reser she made a mystical sign with her open hand, very much like the sign of the cross. Reser responded with an identical gesture. She crossed her hands at the wrists. Promptly, as if anticipating this movement, he did likewise. They now approached each other and, with wrists crossed, shook hands vigorously three times with a downward motion. Then they embraced.

After a rapid conversation in Creole Reser introduced us to her, explaining that she was the *mambo,* the Voodoo priestess. She understood no English, but nodded and smiled as he told her about our interest in the native worship. Her features, cut out of ebony, were sharp and arresting. Her eyes were all-seeing, her movements electric.

"We will go inside," Reser explained. "The service is about to begin."

Obviously he had been here on previous occasions. He greeted the people. Some clasped his hands. I heard his name whispered about in the crowd and decided we were in good company. The glances of the worshipers were no more suspicious or curious than were our own as we familiarized ourselves with the surroundings.

The building was a peristyle, a large palm-thatched canopy with colonnades of hand-hewn poles supporting the edge of the roof and with a single long center pole holding up the peaked apex. Rows of backless benches, set under the rim of the roof, formed a rectangular enclosure about twenty by thirty feet. Here some hundred worshipers were crowded together. The men wore faded, loose-fitting trousers and light-colored shirts, the nondescript clothes of the Haitian peasant. Most of the women were attired in skimpy, shapeless dresses made of unbleached materials. Some wore the large-brimmed peasants' hats, others had white head scarves. Apparently most of the people were barefooted.

The setting for the service had the same informal tone as the worshipers. Built around the center pole was a low altar of brown masonry. On it were candles stuck into the necks of bottles, many earthen pots, a homemade cross, calabash bowls and a gourd covered with a network of multicolored beads and snake vertebrae.

We took our places on a front-row bench, escorted by a girl about fifteen dressed neatly in white and wearing a long strand of beads interwoven with snake vertebrae and sea shells. Six other girls similarly attired stood near by. Reser identified them as the *hounsi-canzo,* the *mambo's* helpers.

My first impression, after I had acquainted myself with the sinisterly lighted surroundings, was a sharply personal one. I began to feel the brooding eyes of the worshipers. Mysterious, fatalistic eyes, accusing, inquiring, vaguely wondering eyes, eyes that sparkled like the unsteady candlelight, eyes that hovered upon us haughtily. Proud, saddened, phlegmatic, tolerant eyes, the eyes of the common people, who see in the dark.

"To understand Voodoo," Reser was saying, "one must enter into the spirit of it. That is true in an appreciation of any faith. Like Ezekiel, we must stand where the people stand. We must become like those who believe."

I could only agree with him there.

"Look at the center pole," he continued. "That is sacred to Damballa, one of the greatest and most prominent of the *loa*. Damballa is represented by a snake, a red boa constrictor. As you look at the pole, imagine that a snake is coiled around it. It isn't there, but it is in your mind. When Christians look at the cross they see a figure hanging there even when there is none. Tonight, visualize Damballa."

I passed the suggestion on to Lorena. We fixed our eyes obediently upon the pole. Others also fastened their attention upon it as if their thoughts, no less than their glances, followed us. A man brought in a feebly burning lantern and tied it to the pole just above the altar as if to provide a focal point for our attention. I thought of a snake, a large red snake. I thought of Damballa, a powerful *loa*. I was all in favor of getting the true believer's point of view.

4.

WHILE the *hounsi* stood by like acolytes waiting, the *mambo* entered with unhurried grace. She moved to the altar and picked up the bead-covered gourd. Reser explained that this was the *asson*, the symbol of priestly office. Raising it in her right hand, the *mambo* shook it vigorously as if blessing in turn the four cardinal points of the peristyle. Attached to the *asson* was a small metal bell which invoked the good *loa* and warded off the evil influences. The ringing of the bell and the rattling of the beads against the gourd gave off mingled sensations of beauty and savage tonelessness. Instantly a low fusillade of drums broke into the scene. Then an *ogan,* steel hitting upon steel, sent out its chilling staccato beat.

The drummers and the *ogantier* were directly across from us, half hidden in the shadows. A young man dressed in faded blue blouse, white pants and a tattered straw hat played the *maman* drum. Next to him sat the *seconde* drummer, a stout middle-aged man with a white kerchief around his forehead. He was banging out his intricate rhythm with one short stick and a small bow held in his right hand in such a way that he could beat either with the flat of his hand or the end of the bow. The man who bent over the *cata* drum was stripped to the waist. An unlighted cigarette dangled from his lips. He tossed his head in a jerky motion in accompaniment to the lightning-fast movement of his hands. Near him stood the *ogantier* holding in his left hand a small steel bar which he tapped with a large iron spike. Each drum had its distinctive rhythm. They blended with the *ogan* into an hypnotic symphony against which I consciously braced myself and into which I was unconsciously drawn. My spirit was already following the *ogan's* inhuman cry and the drums' ghoulish incantation. I was being led out into the night and lured to far-off Dahomey while the *mambo* haunted me with her high-pitched lingering chant.

I could hear Reser involuntarily reciting the words under his breath. In him was recorded the mystery of this unfolding ritual. In him I felt a vibrant response as the *mambo* began to weave her graceful, spinal movement, rattling the *asson* and moving it up and down in snakelike fashion as if invoking the spirits of earth and sky. Reser whispered that she was calling upon Papa Legba, the first *loa* invoked at every service. She was inviting Legba and other saints with a prayer of praise and imploring them to look with favor upon this chosen people.

Reser said, "Three songs are sung during the invocation of each *loa*. The first is always to Legba. Listen! They are saying, 'Papa Legba, open the gate, Papa Legba, open the gate that I may pass. Open the gate so that I may thank the *loa*.' "

I passed this information on to Lorena. I was glad I did, for she was already partially hypnotized by the embrangling sounds and the swaying motion of the worshipers.

"That *mambo!*" Lorena murmured, as if her spirit were slowly dying because she was cameraless.

The *mambo's* body was charged with rhythm. Every muscle quivered. Centuries of jungle dancing pulsed through her. There was a blending of worship and the cabaret. Then, swift as the turn of a thought, she gave the impression of a relaxed freedom emancipating her from toil, custom and restraint. She was the agent of the gods. The white cotton turban was a crown, the *asson*, a scepter, her eyes, jewels. The melody of her movements was the shape and substance of the *loa*.

"God must love rhythm," Reser was saying in a voice absorbed with the spirit of faith. "When He made man He implanted it within him. These people have a double portion of it. Listen to those drums! The staccato *catá, catá, catá* gives the smallest drum its name. The *seconde* takes up the rhythm with its um-pim, pim, um-pim, pim, bid'-dlilip, um-pim, pim. The *maman* drum says boom, boom, pim, pim, boom, boom, bim, bim, bim. Then it breaks in with b-r-r-r-r-r, bang! boom, bang!" The rhythm was in his soul. The drumbeats were infused into the essence of his life.

"Christians," he said, "invoke the spirit with songs and music. Here the drums and the chants and especially the *mambo* are the instruments. The *mambo* is performing her ritual according to prescribed forms. Watch now, every move she makes has special meaning. Oh-o, oh-o, this isn't part of the service. Or is it?"

The *mambo* stood before him. Her eyes swept over him while her body pivoted gracefully. She made several quick signs with the *asson* as if blessing him. Her movements drew him to his feet. He was being invoked to participate in the intricate phases of the ritual, and, obviously, he had been cast in this role many times before.

The *mambo* gave him the *asson* with the bell attached and then presented him with an earthen jar of water. These he accepted in a ceremony in which the *mambo* and he graciously saluted each other. Then they saluted the four points of the compass after which he poured libations in front of the drums, starting with the *ogan* and going in order from *cata* drum to *maman*. Rattling the *asson* he moved to the base of the center pole and poured there three libations.

I glanced around. Pleasure and expectation were written on the faces of the worshipers. Many trembled as if they felt a power generated by the white man and the *mambo* and the swaying *hounsi*. The swift hands of the drummers became faultless mechanisms as their complicated rhythms sprang from deep within their semientranced states. Every bone, every muscle in their bodies was in motion. The *ogantier* held the instrument of steel high in his hands and with his body leaning back, his eyes closed, he banged out his piercing syncopations.

Emotion was rising. The swaying movement ran through the worshipers, the never-ending reverberations of the drums became a steady roar, a rushing as of a mighty wind, which could at any moment fill this jungle peristyle with the spectacular phenomenon of an "upper room." It was like that, an

improvised prologue to a Pentecostal revival, only this performance was entirely ritualistic. It was a ceremonial to the
loa and a litany in Creole and *langage,* the ancient African
dialect which Voodoo deities claim as their mother tongue.

Reser danced with abandon, but always with dignity. His
transfigured expression disclosed deep sincerity, and his dy-
namic movements must have pleased the *loa* as much as they
pleased the people. His affection for Voodoo was evident in
these moments even as it had been in his recitation of the folk
stories and songs and as it had so frequently been when he met
Haitian peasants in country lane or city street. He was a true
envoy of their faith. He was also our surety in our first Voodoo service. I trusted him, and I felt that through him this
audience trusted me. Until I was forced to believe differently
I would act upon this feeling.

Lorena and I leaned forward and gave ourselves over to the
power of the ritual and the incessant chorus of the drums. Only
one thing caused me concern. I wondered what would happen
if Reser should suddenly become possessed by a *loa* and leave
us to shift for ourselves in a revival service more intense and
unpredictable than any of those in which evangelistic Christians
set out to hit the sawdust trail.

5.

IT CAME as a surprise to me that there was
nothing in the opening portion of the service which hinted of
sex or drunkenness. I had anticipated the free use of rum or
clairin by both priestess and participants. Almost every account
I had read had assured me that rum and Voodoo were closely

intermingled. What I had witnessed during the first thirty minutes was a sacrament as old as the human race—a religious dance—and when Reser seated himself beside me on the backless bench in the peristyle he had his own explanation.

"Aristotle was right when he said that the dance is a spiritually imitative act." He spoke with intense satisfaction. "This is liturgy as we see it and feel it. It is nothing new or strange or exclusive in Voodoo to believe that our motion sets the gods in motion. Every true faith has believed that. Miriam knew it when she danced before the Lord. David knew it. The early church knew it. The early church had its exorcists whose business it was to conjure the devil and drive him away with the proper movements and phrases. What I am saying is that Voodoo has its relationship with other religions at every point and draws together all the basic motivations in primitive and modern faiths."

He never allowed this opinion to slip from my mind. Voodoo was the synthesis of the old and new. It stood midway between religion as an obedience to forms, and religion as an individual psychological experience. That is why he found in Voodoo form and spirit, something cosmic, yet personal, something interwoven with the whole of mankind even as the *asson* was interwoven with modern beads and the vertebrae of the snake. Those who missed this universal, all-encompassing meaning saw Voodoo only as escape and superstition.

But now Lorena and I were absorbed by a pageant of preparations which began with the entrance of the *hounsi* bearing multicolored silk flags in procession around the center post. Among the *hounsi* was a man, neatly dressed in white, wearing a white kerchief around his head and carrying a sword upraised in his right hand. Reser identified him as an assistant to the *mambo* and gave him the title of *la place*. To a triumphant roll of the drums, the flags and the sword saluted the post sacred to Damballa, and the vision of the snake was intensified in my mind.

The *mambo* made a motion to one of the *hounsi,* who stepped out of the circle and knelt before her. The *mambo* took a long string of beads and laid it over the *hounsi's* shoulders, then she blessed her with the sign of the cross. The *hounsi* kissed the ground, after which the *mambo* took her by the hand and raised her up. The sanctified one now took a jar of water from the altar, drew a circle of water around the central post and trailed the design off to one of the openings of the peristyle. Here she disappeared in the dark.

Reser explained to us that this magic circle was in honor of Papa Legba and Ogoun Ferreille, the master of the house. Just outside the peristyle, we were told, was another altar upon which were sacred elements soon to be used in the service.

"You would find there bowls of wheat flour and corn meal," Reser said, "leaves and herbs, rum and liqueurs, chickens for the sacrifice, bottles of oil and three kettles, two of baked clay and one of iron. These and other things are in preparation for the great service, *Retrait de l'esprit de l'eau,* the Return of the spirits from below the sea, a preliminary to the purification ceremony, *bruler zin."*

Lorena pressed forward, for we had heard Reser use the words *bruler zin* in connection with *kanzo,* the fire ceremony.

So we watched expectantly as the chosen *hounsi* returned, bearing in her hands a white bowl. She approached the *mambo,* who halted her with an upraised hand. The drums stopped. The encircling figures of the marching *hounsi* and *la place* withdrew from the center of the peristyle and dropped to their

knees. The *mambo,* standing inside the magic circle, beckoned
to the *hounsi* who bore the bowl. Impressively the acolyte advanced. The *mambo* dipped her right hand into the bowl and
took out a small fistful of white meal.

"You will see the making of a *veve,*" Reser whispered. "This,
again, is something that goes back into the primitive past, back
as far as the cabala of the Jews and forward into Catholicism.
A *veve* is a mystical sign. Here, once more, Voodoo stands between the old and the new."

The *mambo* bent down. Permitting the meal to filter between forefinger and thumb, she outlined with smooth, dexterous strokes an artistic design on the peristyle floor. The white
meal against the dark earth stood out sharply as she drew an
unerringly straight line, then she laid another over it to form
a perfect cross. With the same rhythmic motion, she dipped
her hand into the bowl. Again a small ribbon of meal streamed
from her hand to form the outline of a heart.

"She is making the emblem of the *loa* whom she is invoking," Reser explained. "The function of the *veve* is to lead us
nearer to the *loa* and to satisfy a sacrament to the gods. The
mambo stands within the magic circle. Only the good spirits
can approach her."

Under the *mambo's* highly skilled sense of perspective the
veve grew. At the cardinal points of the white cross perfectly
formed hearts appeared, then circles and a lacework of interweaving lines.

"It's totemic," Reser acknowledged almost to himself. "It's
African. It's Indian. It's Greek. It's Christian. It's Voodoo."

With her gaze fixed on the *veve*-making *mambo,* Lorena
whispered her thoughts to me. "I won't leave Haiti until I get
a picture of a *mambo* and a *veve!*"

I could not blame her for that. The stylized drawing was a work of art. The *mambo* had the undivided attention of every observer and it reminded me of the awe that holds a congregation when the priest raises the monstrance in the holy Mass.

"Pythagoras made his *'veve'* with numbers," Reser was saying. "The cabalists used spheres and letters. In Catholicism the bishop takes his pastoral staff and traces signs on the floor of a church which is to be dedicated. It is all part of the same religious impulse. Voodoo *veves* are evidences that the priest or priestess is bona fide. The *mambo* dare not make a mistake. She must know exactly how this symbol is to appear."

"Could you tell if she made a mistake?" Lorena asked.

"Certainly" was the reply. "So can many others here tonight. So can the *loa*."

The *veve* was now a mosaic of complex signs, vivid as a chalk drawing upon a blackboard. Reser whispered, "Damballa," for with dexterous strokes the curving figure of a snake was being outlined with the last remaining handful of meal. Damballa Wedo had been honored and invoked, and now, as the *mambo* stood in an attitude of prayer, the eyes of the worshipers were lowered reverently.

She then intoned a lengthy prayer which was accompanied by the *hounsi* choir. Catholic and Voodoo saints were invoked, and Christian and Voodoo blessings were asked for all who would embark deeper into the mystery of faith. Then the *mambo* said sharply, *"Tamboyué!"* and the drums broke into an ear-shattering salute for Damballa. It was a long roll on the *maman* drum and a series of quick taps on the others, which filled the peristyle with cacophony as a climax to the magic-religious ritual. The *veve,* the center of attention, became the zone of a vital force. By looking at it the worshipers took strength and satisfaction, and upon careful inspection of it Damballa must have been delighted.

The *mambo* picked up the *asson*. In sudden contrast to the fixation of attention on the *veve,* she threw herself into a swaying dance that immediately unleashed the emotions of the spectators. A maze of waltzing figures moved around the altar mingling with the *hounsi* and *la place.* Men and women came from the benches to join this pantomime of praise as if indicating that the symbolism of the *veve* had been understood and that the gods were pleased.

Nearer and nearer to the *veve* edged the dancers. Higher and more frenzied became the holy passion of the participants. The bare feet of the *mambo* touched the corn-meal drawing, then danced upon it, blotting out a portion of the white design. Others followed. Now swiftly moving feet went round and round until the *veve* was entirely stamped out and the meal was ground into the damp earth.

A flood of Creole rose to Reser's lips, expressing his approval. Then turning to us, he spoke in a voice that was exaltedly calm against the excited dancing. "The sign that was made upon the earth," he said, "is now written upon our hearts."

6.

IN THE dim lantern light just outside the peristyle men were tacking a white cloth to a flimsy wooden rigging. Reser, following my glance, said simply, "We are soon to witness the *Retrait de l'esprit de l'eau,* the Return of the spirits from beneath the water."

There was no time for questioning him on the meaning of this, for a sudden transposition from praise to solemn watchfulness caught us in a new spell. The drums marked this shift of mood with a change of rhythm. Those of us who had remained on the benches got up. We were part of the crowd pushing back to make way for the *mambo* followed by *la place* with the sword, flag bearers and a long file of white-clad *hounsi* with their long colorful strands of ceremonial beads. Seven of the *hounsi* bore on their heads cloth-wrapped earthen jars which they steadied with their hands.

"The jars are the sacred *govi*," Reser hurried to explain, "mystical containers prepared to receive the spirits of the dead."

"What is in them?" Lorena asked.

"A bit of wine and rum, an egg and a bit of bread—also mombin leaves and leaves of the lalo-guinin."

The *mambo* was leading her solemnly chanting retinue around the altar and then escorted them out to where the white cloth enclosure had been formed.

"Come," said Reser, "come for the *Retrait de l'esprit de l'eau!*"

The crowd was already moving forward and carrying us out under the open sky. Some of the people made way for our guide so that he could lead us to a close vantage point. Soon we stood before a crude canopy of cloth about six feet long, three or four feet wide and perhaps six feet high. It reminded me of a spiritualist's cabinet in which mediums sit during their entranced states. Reser called it a *card*. He informed us that inside was a tub of water to which had been added wines, liqueurs, small cakes, an egg, leaves of mombin and lalo-guinin, and that the *mambo* had previously made a *veve* of corn meal on the tub. His earnest description and his tone of sincerity transformed the primitive enclosure into an ancient ark of the covenant, designated for special worship in the starlit loveliness of the night.

The seven *hounsi* lay down on the ground in front of the *card* or canopy, each clasping a sacred *govi* in her arms. They lay close together, their bodies touching. Then they were covered completely with a white sheet. This done, the *mambo* stepped inside the *card,* and the flap was fastened down.

In a moment of silence the crowd adjusted itself and waited. The voice of the *mambo* intoned an invocation in Creole. Reser whispered that it was Creole and *langage.* She began calling upon Catholic saints and Voodoo *loa,* and the crowd, led by Reser, responded. This antiphonal exercise took the form of a liturgical prayer, beginning with, *"Gran-Pere Eternel-Diore, rele Gran-Pere Eternal-Dior docrois agoué rele Gran-Pere Eternel si nous nan main, Bon Dieu O Seigneur!"*

This litany was repeated for the various deities, for both Christian saints and African *loa.* On and on went the *mambo's* ancient canticle calling forth a long train of celebrated spirits, saluting the family of heaven for a thirty-minute period in which we stood motionless. A sorcery was spun on the wings of a prolonged incantation, and we were made more conscious of the unseen than the seen. Then the *mambo* called for a *govi.* There was a rustling beneath the sheet, and the hands of a *hounsi* held up a sacred vase. This was passed in to the *mambo.*

We waited in a stillness that was intense. All at once a sound came from inside the cloth enclosure. It was a sudden babbling of water like a brook rushing over stones. Then there was a brief instant of quiet, out of which came a man's voice, deep and gasping.

"He's speaking from the island beneath the sea," Reser said quietly. "The first soul is being released."

The spirit voice speaking in Creole called the name of one of the worshipers. A woman in the crowd responded eagerly.

Then a message came for her veiled by the water's sound. The *mambo* also spoke as if to assure us that she was fully in control of this phenomenon and as if she meant to lure the spirit farther and farther into reality. Reser explained that the departed souls were not only giving messages, but that they were being liberated from their "purgatory" of bondage and assisted in the attainment of a happier, fuller life.

At the end of about five minutes the *govi* was returned to the *hounsi* under the sheet. Each *govi* would, in turn, be presented to the *mambo,* and the spirit of a departed loved one would be conjured from below the water. Each would give messages and advice and go on to its liberation.

This was spiritualism, Voodoo style, with a touch of Catholicism and its masses for the dead. This was direct voice mediumship with special religious implications. The fervor of worship was never lost, the action was never separated from the psychic stream. Intermittent chants, responsories and hymns were part of the ritualistic form. The attitude among the closely gathered spectators, Lorena and I included, was one of reverent attention.

Reser was our interpreter. "Now the spirit is calling for his sister," he said. "Yes, she is here. She is asking about other departed members of the family. Now she wants advice about a family problem. Listen, here is the answer. Oh-o! The *mambo* is reprimanding the spirit and giving *him* some advice!"

The voices "from the dead" and the human voices carried on their dialogues. The assurance of life after death in which every true Christian is expected to believe was here extended to the phenomenon of communication. Perhaps this is what Reser meant when he assured us again that "Voodoo adds knowledge to faith." He believed unquestioningly that these muffled utterances were those of discarnate spirits. Some had been invoked, but others came through by their own striving force, begging to be liberated and asking the *mambo* to take pity upon them and "raise them up."

Reser explained, "There are always some spirits that are 'foreign.' They are clamoring to break through when the psychic contact has been made. It is like tuning in to a field of closely related wave lengths. The *mambo* in this case is the receiving instrument. She 'dials out' the spirits who have no right to come through. However, the spirits for whom no preparation has been made will be called up at a not-distant future, for it is believed that neglected spirits can cause trouble for those who are at fault."

Throughout all this I tried to figure out just how the effect of the voices could be produced. At first I thought that the *mambo* was simply a good ventriloquist. However, this theory proved unlikely because of the wide variety of the vocal effects, and also because the *mambo's* voice and the "voices from beneath the water" frequently spoke simultaneously. I had also suspected that the voices might come from persons concealed in the *card* or from the *hounsi* themselves as they lay under the sheet. These suppositions had to be discarded. Nor was there the possibility of any electrical or sound equipment being employed in this primitive setting. Exposés that had worked in disclosing pseudomediums would not work here.

After going over the possibilities for fraud and deceit, I always came back to one conclusion: either we were hypnotized, or the voices were real. Gradually I became convinced that hypnotism was out, but for me to admit that these were actually the voices of the dead demanded a great amount of credulity.

I glanced questioningly at Lorena to find out what she was thinking. She wrinkled her brow skeptically. Why not believe in this as Reser believed?

He read my thoughts. "This is direct voice communication," he said flatly. "What? You find it hard to agree? Wait and see."

I did not know whether he was referring to the voices which continued to come through the gurgling water or whether he anticipated the exclamations of the *loa* who suddenly began to speak and announced themselves as Loco and Ogoun.

Their "appearing" created a stir of joy among the crowd. The worshipers responded by saying, *"Bonjour,* Papa Loco. *Bonjour,* Papa Ogoun."

"Bonjour, pitite mue yo," answered the *loa.*

The *loa* brought a surge of good feeling to everyone. Reser seemed carried away by the confident assurance that this was a real endorsement of the service.

Voodoo meant many things, but over it all was an impulse toward joy bordering on escape. Just now this might have been a theater audience acclaiming the greetings of its favorite stars. No one entered more fully into the spirit of all this than the white man at our side who happily carried on an intimate conversation with a *loa* to the delight of everyone around. Regardless of what I would later find in Voodoo, despite any personal reaction I might have as to the validity of these mediumistic demonstrations, just now I was ready to admit that Reser had found something thrilling and beneficial in this faith.

A Haitian at our side spoke to us rapturously. I had no idea what he was saying, but Reser came to the rescue.

"He wants to know how you like this" was Reser's interpretation. "He says that these things are not miraculous. God works this way."

All the while the voices of the *loa* were in the air, and the words of the spirits from beneath the sea filled the night with festivity. Finally the flap of the *card* opened, and the *mambo* stepped out. She looked very tired, but as the *hounsi* arose from beneath the sheets and as the people greeted her she smiled and revived. As she led the procession back to the peristyle the syncopated throb of the drums aroused within her a latent fire. Her steps became a dancing pattern. She intoned a chant. Her voice matched the dull hammering of the drums. The geometrical sway of her body made the worshipers breathe in an exotic rhythm.

We were caught in the strong surge of a Voodoo spell. We had been standing for more than two hours. Now there was rapturous movement and life. Now the drums were beating, and the scene was poetic with motion. Reverently the seven *hounsi* placed the *govis* upon the altar. Then the people stepped back, for now in the clearing three fires were being kindled on the peristyle ground.

Reser said solemnly, "The time has come for the fire ceremony, *bruler zin.*"

7.

THE *hounsi-canzo* brought in bottles of oil, earthen bowls and two live chickens. Three men followed them, each bearing a *zin* or kettle. Led by *la place,* this group circled the center pole while the drums banged and the *mambo* rattled the *asson*.

I could feel the service rising to a feverish pitch. Voodoo's relationship to the Christian religion was deepening. A sacrifice was being called for. Around me black people laughed and talked and trembled expectantly. Beside me sat a white man who saw and felt symbolism in every move and meaning in every act.

"One of the two *zins* of baked clay is for the living and the other is for the dead," he explained. "The iron one bears the emblem of Ogoun Ferreille, the ironworker. It is a Nago *zin*."

The *hounsi* with the chickens came to the *mambo* and bowed down. The *mambo* took the chickens. The *hounsi* knelt down and kissed the ground. Deftly holding a chicken in each hand, the *mambo* presented them solemnly in turn to the east, west, north and south. Then she touched the chickens to the body of each *hounsi* as if indicating that through this offering the spirits of her assistants were making their own willing sacrifice to the deities. Reser nudged me, calling my attention to the fact that the fires were being lighted and that men had driven large iron spikes into the ground at the rim of the flames. These spikes would support the *zins* or kettles.

The congregation sang, *"Ogoun Badagri, map planté pateau é!"* (Ogoun Badagri, I am going to plant the post.)

The chorus of voices seemed to be joined by a choir of *loa* from the island beneath the sea. The peristyle throbbed with the singing. The fires grew. The spikes were pounded down. Kola, liqueurs, finely cut fruit, roasted corn and peanuts were scattered on and around the spikes.

Then the *mambo* held the chickens with their beaks close to the ground while the drums grumbled their incoherent pleas. The chanting stopped. The people waited. Why was this moment so intense? Why was this act so meaningful? The chickens seemed to shudder for an instant, and then they picked greedily at the offerings near the fire.

"See that!" Reser exclaimed. "They are now signifying their willingness to die!" The words were like the death sentence for a living soul.

I glanced at him. His face was immobile. His eyes were half closed. He looked Negroid. He was seeing something I did not see. His thoughts had gone beyond mine.

The *mambo* returned the chickens to the *hounsi* who held them in outstretched hands. It now occurred to me that these chickens were in a state of trance or hypnosis. They no longer fluttered. Their heads were stretched out as if in fright. Their throbbing bodies seemed to keep time with the accelerated beat of the drums. Perhaps they, too, saw death.

Solemnly the *mambo* took a bottle from the *hounsi* and poured oil on the spikes and on the flames. The *hounsi* dropped mombin leaves on the fire. The flames rose over the candles and filled the peristyle with a great light. Leaning forward as if welcoming this brightness the congregation sat lost in a deeply religious experience. The drummers punctuated their rhythm with emphatic shouts. Their faces glistening with sweat, they were losing themselves more and more in their faultless performance. Their bodies swayed, their heads swung back in ecstasy. Every muscle was attuned to the intrepid action of their flying hands.

The *zins* were set in place. Once more the *mambo* took the chickens. Again she presented them to the four cardinal points.

Then with a quick motion she broke the chickens' legs. Swiftly, in turn, she opened their beaks, thrust in a finger and broke a carotid. Now she plucked a few feathers from their necks, caught some blood on the feathers and made rapid mystical signs over the *zins* and the altar. A little blood was dropped into the *govi*.

All of this was done with stark precision. All was watched intently, as if the people knew whether or not it was in keeping with the ritual. Meanwhile the flames had burned over the *zins* and blackened them.

Reser was supersensitive to my feeling. "Blood sacrifice," he said, "is no isolated phenomenon. It goes on all over the world. It was known to every religion, though some have forgotten it."

The chickens were now given to two men who quickly plucked them and threw their feathers and entrails into the flames, scattering a few feathers on the spikes and on the mouths of the pots. Water was then poured into the iron *zin,* and the cleaned chickens were dropped in. Here they were quickly cooked and then removed. Corn meal was also cooked, removed with a wooden spoon, molded into balls and dropped into the mombin leaves. Now oil was poured into the earthen *zins.*

"That oil," Reser explained, "must catch fire inside those kettles or the service is no success."

He meant the gods would be displeased. So we watched while the fire licked at the sides of the kettles, and we felt like applauding when the flames crept up close to the rims. It was like viewing an exciting play. The whole assemblage sat like chiseled figures while the drums kept up their ceaseless, unchanging drone and the *mambo* rattled the *asson*. The air was thick with the smell of burning feathers and the pungent scent of pine.

When the *hounsi* started a song Reser joined in with the singing. It seemed to me that they were conjuring the flames so that they would break over into the oil and drive away whatever evil forces held back the fire. The suspense increased. One of the assistants poured rum into the flames. The fire shot up in an inferno of blue and red. There were low exclamations from the worshipers. Some started a swaying motion. The fire receded. The evil spirits seemed to be winning. The flames were dying. The *mambo* walked majestically to the *zins* and stood for a moment looking down. Then she made a mystical sign. The flames rose as if in answer to her appeal. Suddenly they rolled into the oil, making the *zins* two fiery caldrons burning inside and out while the drums vied with the people in triumphant acclaim.

La place and the flag-bearers, joined by the *hounsi,* paraded around the altar and the fires. As I watched them I caught sight of two young men, barefooted, attired in short pants and loose-fitting sleeveless shirts. They had entered unobserved, and I turned questioningly to Reser.

"*Hounsi-canzo,*" he said. "Members of the families whose *zins* are being burned. What they will do is in the nature of the renewal of a sacrament."

Lorena clutched my arm as the men fell to their knees in front of the wildly burning *zins*. Here they knelt as the *mambo* blessed them. Turning directly toward the fire, each in front of an earthen *zin,* the young men held out their arms to the flames.

"They will put their hands into the fire," Reser stated.

I looked around the peristyle, for it had grown so still and the drums were beating so softly that all seemed strangely unreal. The black forms of the Voodooists were jammed together. Some stood on the benches, and a number of children hung on the poles at the edges of the peristyle. The *hounsi* and the flag-bearers, *la place* and the omnipotent *mambo* waited. The earth was trembling under the muffled-staccato rifle shots of the drums. The sudden rise and fall of the litany sounded as intricate as a Gregorian chant and as impending as a storm. My eyes were burning with the heat of the fire. My throat was choking with the scent of burning things.

Together the two men thrust their hands into the flames. They held them there deliberately, as if to prove to us that this was real. They did not flinch. They made no cry. They showed no sign of pain.

Time stopped while we watched this spectacle. It seemed like an eternity before they drew away from the crackling fire, only to fall back on their shoulders and put their feet into the flames. I closed my eyes to bring myself back to reality. I looked again and saw the men on their knees holding out their unscarred hands to the *mambo*. She nodded and smiled. Their faces remained set, and their eyes were gentle; so gentle, in fact, was their whole demeanor that the audience looked at them quietly without applause.

"They were ready for it," Reser observed. "Their training had prepared them well."

I turned to him, for his voice was as casual as if he were commenting on the most commonplace of happenings.

Then, as a reverent procession formed to lead these two *hounsi-canzo* away, Reser touched my arm and quoted, " 'Steadily, unflinchingly, we strive to pierce the inmost heart of nature. Veil after veil is lifted and her face grows more beautiful and wonderful with every barrier that is withdrawn.' "

8.

THE service was over. The last of the fire was beaten out with mombin branches and the ground swept clean. The balls of food, a spoon and a knife were wrapped in a new white napkin. This, in turn, was folded into a white tablecloth. The earthen pots were broken into small pieces, and the *mambo* made a circle in a far corner of the peristyle. A hole was dug inside this circle, and the wrapped food and broken kettles were buried in a grave of mombin leaves. The *hounsi* gathered around the hole, pushed the dirt in and tamped it down by dancing on it to the tune of *"Ja relé Ja—Ja O relé Ja!"*

This, Reser explained, was a favorite song of the Guedé people. The words, which defied translation, stuck in our minds while the *mambo* traced another circle over the thoroughly tamped spot. Then she drew a cross inside the circle and placed a lighted candle in the center which was to be left there to burn itself out.

The moon was up. Through the tropical silver of the night the worshipers made their unhurried departure from the peristyle. We were as reluctant to go as the rest, for the *mambo* and Reser were discussing the events of the evening. Up to now, Voodoo had not proved to be cannibalism or black magic. We were haunted by a feeling of reverence and awe. The voices of the "spirits from beneath the sea" lingered in my memory.

The *kanzo* ceremony played havoc with my will to believe but put upon me an indelible impression of something mysterious and unknown.

I had a question. I asked it after we said our good-by to the *mambo* and were once more walking over the rough terrain. "Is it possible," I wanted to know, "that some protective chemical was used on the arms and hands of those men?"

He stopped and looked at me. His voice was pity and pain as he said, "Man, don't you trust your eyes?"

"Well," I had to say, "I didn't examine them."

"You can do so next time," he replied. Then as he started forward, he added, "I wish you had been around and had examined my arms and my hands."

"Yours?" said Lorena quickly. "When?"

"When I took *kanzo*" was the cryptic reply.

"You—went through the *kanzo* ceremony?" I asked.

He took a deep, jealous breath of the scented air. He extended his hands to the beautiful night as if he were once more stretching them over the fire, but I imagined he was welcoming Haiti all over again. With eyes lifted to the brilliant moonlight he said, "The pearl of great price. Yes, when a man has that——"

"*Kanzo*," I prodded. "Isn't it true that anyone who takes *kanzo* is well on his way to becoming a Voodoo priest?"

"That's right," he agreed, and his words were final.

I looked at him through new eyes, and Lorena looked at me. Who was this man, and what were his powers? How much did he know about the mystery lurking behind *kanzo* and the voices from the dead? What would he tell us? What would he let us see?

"The outward ceremony," he was saying, "is the visible form

of the inner reality. There is a baptism of fire that spectators do not see. That is the real thing. Putting one's hands in the fire is only the symbol of putting one's life into harmony with the unseen. Always look for the secret of Voodoo *within.*"

"Within what?" Lorena wanted to know.

"Within the outward signs," he maintained. "Within the inner life. I can give you an idea." He stopped and took a small white stone from his pocket. He laid it in the palm of his hand. The moonlight showed it to be about three inches long, a flattened oval with a brown line in the form of a crescent at one end. As we looked at it closely he said, "This looks like quite an ordinary stone. Actually it is a *pierre loa,* a stone in which the *loa* has chosen to reside in a special way."

"How do you know?" Lorena asked.

"The faithful know. What more can be said?"

"Where did you get it?"

"One night, on a moonlit night very much like this, I was alone in my room getting ready for bed. Something told me to be very still and to meditate upon the *loa.* I sat on the edge of the bed. The presence of some good spirit was very near to me. I could feel it. Suddenly I heard a clicking sound, and beside me lay this stone. This happened on a Thursday night. Sunday night I attended a service, and a woman became possessed of Erzilie. She is one of the greatest *loa,* to us much like the Virgin Mary. Erzilie said to me, 'Are you pleased with the little present I gave you?' I said, 'I would be pleased with anything you might have for me.' She said, 'I mean the little stone I gave you on Thursday evening in your room. When you see it, remember me.'"

His voice was gentle and believing. He turned the stone over in his hand and gazed at it long and fixedly. Then his hand closed over it, for we were startled by a yellow light flashing in our direction.

"Oh-o!" Reser said with a laugh. "It's our car. You see what sharp eyes these people have? Our driver must have seen us way off there in the distance." Then as an afterthought he added, "Or maybe he didn't see us. Maybe Erzilie told him we were coming."

He slipped the *pierre loa* into his pocket and led us forward with confident strides.

Chapter 3

WE BEGAN TO SEE HAITI AND VOO-
doo through Reser's eyes. Whenever we were with him something unusual was bound to happen. I came to expect it. Sometimes it was a little thing, as on the day he stopped to express
his sympathy at a home where a death had occurred. He had
planned to stay only a moment, but the mourners crowding the
house would not let him get away. A wake is the time for story-
telling, cardplaying and singing hymns and litanies to the
saints. Reser was in his element. A woman, who had been
crying copiously for some time and was now wailing as though
her heart would break, caught sight of him through her tears.

"Ah, *M'sieur* Reser," she said in Creole, getting up heavily
from her knees, "come and cry in my place while I go home
and fix myself some lunch!"

He was always happy to oblige, whether it was mourning for
the dead or singing for the living. Walking the streets of Port-
au-Prince with him was like running an obstacle course. Everyone from market peasant to businessman knew him. On Satur-
days, beggars' day in the capital city, he was recognized as a
trusted friend by those who went from door to door for pen-

nies. I had the feeling they were as grateful for his friendship
as for his gifts, and I was about ready to agree with him that
his position among the natives was a fulfillment of prophecy.

"Every life is a mosaic," he philosophized, "but not all
show as perfect a pattern as mine. Why did my old grand-
mother in Utah teach me French instead of English when I
was a boy? Why did I never forget it? God had Haiti written
behind my name. Why was I always reading about religion?
Why did something tell me that the basic principle about God
could not be corralled in any one group? Why did I always
believe that God has no racial prejudice? And when I was a
small boy, why did I cry when Father killed a pet snake, a rat-
tler? I used to feed it milk. I loved that snake."

I thought of Damballa.

"Destiny prepared me," he insisted. "Mother was a musician.
Father called the rounds for square dances. There is no rhythm
I haven't heard. Fate led me to the Alaska-Yukon-Pacific Exposition in 1909. In the Negrito village I heard primitive drumbeats for the first time. They stuck in my mind. They came
out at my finger tips. I heard them again in the South Seas.
I heard them at Sierra Leone outside of Freetown in Africa. In
them was a universality which expressed something native and
vital within all people. Anyone who follows the beat of a drum
will never rest until he rests in Haiti."

Then there was another factor which he insisted was part of
the providential plot. "From boyhood my nickname had been
Doc. I knew the names of all the bones in the human body
before I was ten. When I joined the navy I said to the examining physician, 'Doctor, what does this auscultation tell you?'
Why did I say that? It was that one word that caused the doctor

to help me get into the Hospital Corps, and my medical career began."

His knowledge of medicine was the key that unlocked many Haitian doors for him, including Voodoo. When he conducted country clinics during his days with the Marine Medical Corps in north Haiti, he recommended the use of native cures as well as those of accepted medical practice. He led sanitary-inspection crews on horseback into the jungles, but he never despised the advice of *bocors*. He fought malaria, yaws, intestinal parasites with what he called "mass treatment" at free clinics and post stations. Those associated with him admitted he got results but complained that he worked by "hunches more than method," that he was "more black than white" in his relationship with the people and that he had secrets which he guarded jealously from "white intruders."

All of this was part of the mosaic. I began to suspect that the reports were all true. To me, he seemed like a man who had made a pact with the *loa*. They were more real to him than flesh and blood. His life was peopled with the *mystère*. They were the go-betweens in his relationship with the natives. I was convinced that he worked through these unseen intermediaries to bring about a parapsychical influence of a high order, and things began to happen that could hardly be explained in any other way.

He sat one evening on the porch of the Leonard Thompson home. The American vice-consul was entertaining friends. Next to Reser sat a woman from Jamaica, a Mrs. Mackay. They had been talking about the *loa* when Reser suddenly said, "I get the impression of billows of smoke and flames."

Mrs. Mackay was amused. "Is that Voodoo talk?"

Reser continued, "I get the impression of a house on a sloping lawn surrounded by coconut trees."

"That," said Mrs. Mackay, "could be my house in Jamaica."

"I see smoke and flames at the rear of the house. It is not the house that is burning. It is a shed behind the house."

"You had me frightened for a moment!" Mrs. Mackay exclaimed. "Now I know what it is. That fire happened just a year ago today. I must have been thinking about it unconsciously. You must have read my thoughts."

"The shed burned to the ground," Reser reported.

"It did," she agreed. "My son was cleaning his motorcycle. He had been smoking, and in a few moments the shed was in flames. Tell me more. What else do you see?"

"I see a living room," Reser went on, "with a large chest of drawers and a piece of white wood in the center where one would ordinarily find a mirror. There are papers in the bottom drawer. The room is smaller than it was originally."

"That is all correct!" said Mrs. Mackay. "When my daughter married we partitioned off part of the room to provide for her and her husband."

Just then the vice-consul came from the house. "Excuse me, Mr. Thompson," Reser spoke up. "I get an impression of a home with a large porch and columns and a little pond in the yard. I get the name 'Two Trees Pond.' Does that mean anything to you?"

"Why, yes," said Thompson. "That is my uncle's place in New Jersey. Where did you hear about it?"

"I didn't hear about it. I just now got the impression." Then turning abruptly to a man sitting at his left, he asked, "By the way, sir, do you have a letter in your pocket signed, 'Affectionately, John'?"

"I do not," said the man, getting up and walking away. In a moment he stopped and swung around. "By Jove!" he shouted. "I do have a letter like that! I left it in my desk before coming here. This is most extraordinary. How do you explain it?"

"I don't explain it," Reser said with a shrug. "It was just impressed upon me."

"Do you call this the work of the *loa?*" asked Mrs. Mackay.

"I call it the weight of proof of the existence of an extra-sensory force" was the reply. "It happens that it works excellently in Haiti! The island is rich in this kind of thing. Voodoo is full of it."

Laughing quietly Reser said to me, "Isn't it remarkable how intelligent people are surprised at ordinary examples of super-sensory demonstration and how naturally the so-called primitive mind accepts these phenomena? That is what makes Voodoo so wonderful. It has the faith that these things and greater things shall be done and it expects them. The miracle would be if these things did *not* happen. Remember what the man said to you at the *Retrait de l'esprit de l'eau?* 'These things are not miraculous. God works this way.'"

"You say that Voodoo is full of this type of thing. I want to see more of it."

"You will," he answered. "Only don't ask for it. It might not be what you want."

"Which is to say . . . ?"

He shrugged. "Never tempt the *loa* or trifle with them." Then he tempered this serious pronouncement by adding, "A woman once came to me insisting that she see something or hear something. 'I'll let you hear something,' I told her. 'You have three children, but if your husband had asked me that, I'd have answered him differently!' "

He became philosophical. "Extrasensory perception and pre-cognition are elementary in Voodoo, but they accomplish a function which is highly important in the realm of faith. In your so-called civilized communities, church doctrines are pure-ly academic. A person is taught to believe without evidence. In Voodoo one expects and finds proof of the things he is taught. If faith is believing in things unseen, then Voodoo goes beyond faith. It believes and then demonstrates that the belief is true."

He gave his testimony: "I was visiting with friends one day when a woman from the neighborhood came up possessed by Papa Ogoun, a *loa* who travels great distances and is compar-able to St. James the Greater. He was the one who converted the magician Hermogenes because James was a better magician with God on his side than Hermogenes was with the devil on his! And Papa Ogoun is just as great as James. It was Papa Ogoun's day, Wednesday, that the woman was possessed. She was wearing red, Ogoun's color, and Ogoun had entered her head. 'Look!' said Ogoun to three guests standing with me in the yard, 'On the tenth day from today these things are going to happen to you, and to you, and to you!' Pointing to each one, Ogoun said, 'In ten days you, Tazi, are going to have a big quarrel in your family. In ten days you, Justin, are going to get a letter that will bring you into court. In ten days you, Tite, are going to have a bad fall and you must lie in bed.' "

"And—in ten days?"

"I made it my business to investigate," said Reser. "On the

tenth day I went to Tazi's home. She was a widow supported by two daughters who sold charcoal. When I came up the path I heard a terrible row. Tazi's brothers had torn down her fence so that their goats could come in and eat the grass. The animals had chewed up the cowpeas and the garden stuff, and now Tazi was having her say. At one o'clock on this same day a car drove up and presented Justin with a summons. He owed a man 175 gourdes and was hauled off to court. Nothing had happened to Tite. That evening she came to my house as if to show me that her part of the prophecy had not come true. She stayed until after dark. On the way home she took a short cut through the garden under the mango trees and through the sugar cane. The men had been irrigating, and the water had overflowed the banks. Tite came to a low place and tried to jump over. She slipped and struck her back on a stump. She was able to hobble home, but had to remain in bed for ten days."

"Coincidence?" I asked. "Or maybe the power of suggestion?"

"Take your choice" was the shrugging reply. "The time element was right. The predictions were right. The mathematical chances that it might have been a coincidence are astronomical. It was the work of the *loa*—in this case, Papa Ogoun. With them, as with all spiritual forces, past, present and future are coexistent. We shall have to rethink our whole relationship with the Power that governs the universe. If your cultured faiths cannot get people to do this, Voodoo will."

He always came back to that: Voodoo has something to offer the world. Voodoo is the link between primitive and modern religion. Voodoo is the catalyst. The *loa* reaches out to unite man to cosmic force.

Reser was *loa*-conscious. I came upon him one day unobserved and found him staring fixedly into a glass of water. He said he often saw figures in the water and had things revealed to him that way. I was with him one dark night when he accidentally stepped off a porch into space and fell eight feet to the ground, barely missing some jagged stones. Uninjured but for a small scratch on his arm, he said that the *loa* had protected him. One evening I snapped his picture with a Polaroid camera. When I took the print from the case it showed a white cloud hovering over his head. Under a magnifying glass this "ectoplasmic mist" revealed four distinct faces. He said they were pictures of *loa* and suggested their names.

One day a friend brought him a crystal ball. He found it worked better than the glass of water. He held it under his unvarying gaze and announced that he saw a coffin completely covered with floral wreaths. "Behind the coffin is a long French mirror. At the right are three chairs. At the left is a row of chairs. Against the right wall is a chaise longue."

Two weeks later to the day he was in a *café* talking with a flier by the name of Jack Harris. Harris said, "I don't want the reputation of being the best flier, but I'd like to be called the oldest!"

Then Harris turned to Homer Howell, an American much loved in north Haiti, and asked whether he would like to see Port-de-Paix from the air. Reser rode out to the airfield with the two men.

While Harris was warming up the engine Howell called Reser to his side under a bayahonda tree and said, "Doc, I want you to do something for me. Give this billfold to Mrs. Bunkley for Tivita." Tivita was Howell's wife. Mrs. Bunkley was the wife of the resident navy doctor. Reser put the billfold into his pocket.

For a reason which will never be known Harris and Howell stunted over the field for twenty minutes. Then they circled the field twice. At the beginning of the third turn the engine cut out and black smoke belched from the plane. It crashed from a height of six hundred feet. Howell's body was thrown from the plane; Harris perished in the wreckage.

The night before the funeral Reser was awakened by a voice. He heard the throaty whisper of the spirit of Homer Howell saying, "Tell Tivita not to worry."

On the following day Reser went to the Howell home and saw the identical scene which had been revealed to him when he gazed into the crystal ball. It was all there—the coffin, the chairs, the French mirror, the chaise longue.

The *loa*—at least two hundred of them—are important in Voodoo lore, and I began to believe that this white Haitian was on speaking terms with them all.

"There is but one God," he said, "but He has infinite ways of expression. He is the *Gran Mait,* imminent and transcendent. He is in the universe and behind the universe. By Him all things are made and in Him all things exist. He is primal cause and ultimate effect. One never gets very close to Him in this life, but there are always the *loa* who help us in our relationship with Him."

"Are all *loa* good?" I asked. "Or can a man sell his soul to a bad *loa* as Faust did?"

"There are good *loa* and evil, just as there are good people and bad. They are like sparks from the divine anvil broken off when the *Gran Mait* fashioned the universe. A man can choose the good or bad *loa,* just as he can choose good or bad companions. It is up to him."

He made it clear that each *loa* has its individual characteristics and each reveals himself or herself consistently according to type. The *houngan* always knows. The *houngan* can always tell which is good and which is evil.

"You will see the *loa,*" he promised. "You will know what I mean. There are whole families of *loa* in the Voodoo pantheon. The Rada *loa* take their name from Arada, people of Dahomey, Africa. They include Damballa, Erzilie Freda, Agué, Baron la Croix, Guedé, Legba, Ogoun and many more. Petro *loa* are Haitian—Simbi Gallone, Mait Kalfu, Petro, Gran Siligbo. There are Ibo *loa* of the kind you saw in the house along the trail near the Chez Pauline. Also Moundougue *loa,* Caplao and others. They are the invisible rulers of the land and the unseen companions of the people. They are near to us. Very near."

So near that one night I could have reached out and touched one.

At a public dance the drummer was Reser's laundress' husband, an unusually big man of quick temper. Toward the close of the evening an old man wandered in and said to the drummer, "Let me play a round or two."

The big man said, "No. Get out of here."

The old man pleaded, but the drummer seized him by the shoulders, turned him around and kicked him. The old man stood quietly for a moment, and in that instant Reser saw something in the stranger's face that made him gasp.

"I have lived over seventy years," said the old man, "and this is the first time anyone has ever kicked me like a donkey. That cannot be. That cannot be." Shaking a finger at the drummer he added, "I am the last man you are ever going to kick."

Those who heard him pleaded, "Don't talk like that. Come and have a drink. Come and forget it."

"Sure," said the man. "I'll have a drink. Why not?"

The following morning the drummer tried to stand and could not. His foot began to swell, and by night the swelling had extended up his leg. There was no mark of infection, no break in the skin, but he cried out in pain. Medication was useless. Doctors could do no good. Reser could do nothing. The *loa* had spoken. The drummer had no protection, no *garde,* no charm to aid him. The next day he died. This was the spell of the *loa,* the never-ending mystery and magic that hung over the island.

More and more I was beginning to learn that Reser—he who had taken *kanzo*—was closer to the source of Voodoo power than I had dreamed. He linked it with a classical reference and quoted from Homer to say, " 'The gods, in the likeness of strangers from far countries, put on all manner of shapes, and wander through the cities, beholding the violence and the righteousness of men.' "

2.

THE *loa* came even nearer on the day we went with Reser to the Plaine du Cul de Sac and a place called Pont Beudet. Here stood the asylum for the insane, the institution of which Reser had at one time been superintendent. The building had originally been built by American Marines as a training post for recruits when they formed the Haitian *Gendarmerie.* The practice for some years had been to confine the troublesome and dangerously insane in the state prisons. Finally they became so numerous that the authorities decided the insane should be treated as patients rather than as prisoners. Nearly three hundred insane had been fed, clothed and treated daily at Pont Beudet during Reser's twelve years of service.

As we paused on the dusty roadside that skirted the drab, neglected buildings Reser said, "Things were different when I was here. The fence wasn't broken down, and the jungle wasn't threatening to take over in those days. Furthermore, the inmates didn't look like that."

He indicated a group of wretchedly clad men moving about the compound. Desolation stretched out around them, out into the swamps and thickets. Even the road was deserted, save for a few scrawny pigs, instead of the usual moving line of burden-bearing, market-bound natives.

"That place taught me a lot," Reser recalled as he sadly viewed the surroundings. "In helping others I found myself. Some of the white population, when they heard I was coming out here, asked, 'You think those gunnies are human? Why are you going?' I'll tell you why. The *loa*. I had been told by a *mambo* that I would come and that is how it worked out. Miracles happened, if you want to call them miracles. There was a man who hadn't walked for many years. He walked."

"Through treatment?"

"Through recognizing that supposed insanity is in reality often a case of possession. By recognizing the *loa* in question and furnishing whatever the *loa* requires, miracle cures can be wrought."

He cited an example. "One Monday morning while I was making my rounds I noticed a woman who had been admitted during the week end. I was told that she had become very violent while at home and that she had created a near panic in the neighborhood. When I saw her she was pacing back and forth, had a wild look in her eyes and was alternately humming and whistling. I called for a *cruche* of water, poured a libation before the door and offered her a cigar. She stopped dead in her tracks and looked at me. Her hand reached out for the cigar and I lighted it for her. Without preamble I asked a question in Creole: 'When are you going to release your horse?' The *loa* in her answered and said, 'When she gives me the food she owes me.'"

"Which *loa* was using her as 'his horse'?" I asked.

"Ogoun."

"How did you know?"

"How does a doctor know which disease is affecting his patient?"

"In this case, Voodoo diagnosis?" I asked.

"And Voodoo cure," he asserted. "I bought a red rooster, corn and peanuts, plantains, sweet potatoes and a yam. Also a bottle of rum. I had it all ritually prepared in her presence, and when Ogoun had accepted it and eaten it to his satisfaction the woman came to herself. She was cured."

"That's what you mean when you say that many cases of insanity are really cases of possession?"

"Certainly. Many people who are brought here have offended the *loa.* Or would you rather call it sin or psychological error? I'm in Haiti. I call it offense against the *loa.* Correct the cause and you have effected the cure. The more a person's character is in opposition to the *loa,* the more violently he fights them. There comes a time when something has to *give.* Either a person goes down to frenzy or up to ecstasy. It's the same path, but it leads both ways, if you know what I mean. The cause that can result in demoniacal attacks in a *loa bossale*—a person who has not been baptized—can result in a sublime experience for one who has been. You see, when a *loa* enters a person for the first time, or 'mounts him,' as the local expression is, a baptismal ceremony is required. This causes the possessed one to have the proper receptivity. That's where the ceremonies and the ritual play their part. That is where the *houngan* comes in."

Lorena and I walked with him along the melancholy road.

"Someday," he prophesied, "men who deal in these cases will learn what every Voodoo priest knows instinctively. The obsessing personality is a distinct personality and can be talked to, reasoned with, influenced and understood. When men understand spiritual psychology they will finally get at the root causes of these things."

In sudden happy recollection, he burst out with a hearty *"Ai-yai-yai!* If you had only been here in those days. You know who used to be my butcher out here? Cicéron. Haiti's greatest drummer. You know why he did the butchering? That was one way he could get just the right hides for his drumheads! I loved that man. I loved these people. Every one of them. Through good treatment and good food and understanding of the *loa* many got better. I always felt the nearness of the *loa* out here at Pont Beudet."

We were now opposite the asylum buildings. A group of inmates huddled against the gray stone wall a short distance from us. Their black, soulless faces were half shielded by their hands as if to ward off our inquiring gaze. Their garments appeared to be sackcloth draped over their wasted bodies. Reser did not pause. He had no intention of entering the grounds. I do not think he even looked at the inmates, but suddenly he was stopped by the sound of his name. An elderly man in the group threw up his arms and began running in our direction, followed by the catapulting forms of three companions.

"Doc! Doc Reser!"

Reser viewed the stumbling old man compassionately. "He knows me," he said with a choke in his voice. "After all these years he still remembers me."

The man crawled through the tangled wire and threw himself to his knees, grasping Reser's hand in both of his. His black face twitched, and he murmured childishly. A tremor passed through his frail body. Reser called him by name and urged him gently to his feet.

Lorena withdrew unobserved and from about twenty feet away hurriedly snapped several pictures, the first she had taken of our guide without his permission. I held my breath wondering what Reser would say, but he made no comment. Apparently he had not noticed or heard the click of the shutter. He was holding the old man's gaze with a fixed stare. Speaking to him in Creole, he was transforming him into a different personality. I would have called it hypnotism back home, but since I was in Haiti, what was I to say? A man, seemingly bereft of reason a few moments ago, shivering with cowardly fright, was becoming a person with a show of self-respect. He began to talk coherently. He began thinking, feeling and acting with a noticeable degree of understanding. The singing stream of Creole with which Reser held him was like healing water. The man looked at his toilworn hands as if seeing them for the first time. He touched them to the gray stubble of his face, conscious of his appearance. A light of illumination drove the tired sadness from his eyes. He brought the palms of his hands together slowly as if in grateful prayer. Even the vacant stares of the three who huddled in the grass at the side of the road took on a show of interest. The man who now stood before Reser appeared to be the real man, his former self only a shadowy counterfeit.

How long this transfiguration would last I did not know. The real man talked and smoked a cigarette and at length walked slowly and thoughtfully back to the compound.

"What will happen to him now?" I asked.

"Why?"

"He looks like a changed man."

"He is."

"And now?"

"He's in good hands," Reser said in utmost confidence.

"You mean the *loa?*"

"I told you they were near to me at Pont Beudet."

Then he told us the story of something that happened during his superintendency. In the light of what I had just seen I believed it. I call it *"La Femme Sans Nom"*—"The Woman Without a Name."

She was in her early twenties and had been brought to Pont Beudet by gendarmes of Port-au-Prince. They said she was crazy. She had been picked up walking naked in the city streets. They wrapped a blanket around her, and she tore it off. They put clothes on her; she ripped them to shreds. So they brought her to the madhouse under guard.

Reser put her in the first cell in the cell block. For three days and nights she crouched in a corner, brooding, suspicious of every sound. It was as if her legs were paralyzed, for she no longer walked or moved about.

The matrons brought their reports to Reser. "She will not wear any clothes. She tears them off and throws them back at us. She says, 'These are not mine!'"

The guards added their complaint. "She has torn up the straw mat with her hands and teeth. Tonight she is sleeping on the stone floor."

Days went by, and the woman without a name was given a place in the women's hospital barracks. She had no visitors. Reser's inquiries about missing persons produced no results. The streets often gave up people who could not be traced. The crowded streets of Port-au-Prince had many homeless wanderers.

Weeks passed. The imperceptible change of tropical seasons touched the wire enclosure of Pont Beudet but never brought reality to its mysterious inmate. From her tangled, changeless world she looked out on the continuously complicated puzzle of existence.

Reser was solicitous. "How are you today? Is there anything we can do for you? Who are you?"

Sometimes she looked at him as if to answer. Sometimes her lips moved, but she never spoke.

One morning the matron hurried into Reser's office. "You know, *Docteur,* that woman danced last night!"

"She did what?"

"She danced."

"Has this happened before?"

"No."

"If it ever happens again, let me know. Call me wherever I may be and no matter what I am doing."

"Yes, *Docteur.*"

A week passed, and then one night Reser awoke in his room

with a start. He felt as if someone had called him by name. He awoke fully, instantly, and a voice ordered him to get dressed. He had often inspected the grounds at night and checked on the guards. But this night when he got outside he wondered why he had been called. The grounds were perfectly silent. Everything had a feeling of order. Everything felt right, but something guided him to the women's hospital barracks. He went in and found the woman without a name sitting on a bench fully dressed. On each side of her was a matron. They were startled at his entrance, but the woman simply looked at him and nodded. Then she spoke. "Didn't I tell you he would come? Didn't I tell you?"

One of the matrons said, "She is possessed by the *loa* Kalfu. He said we should take him to you. We told him we could not because it is against the rules for us to leave at this hour. He said, 'All right, if you won't take me to him, I'll bring him here!'"

Reser dismissed the matrons. Then he said, "What is it, Kalfu? What's the matter with the girl?"

"Nothing the matter with her," said the *"loa."* "She is a thief. I had a beautiful robe. She tore it. I had a chicken. She stole it. I had fifty-four cents. She spent it."

"All right, so she stole your money and your chicken and she tore your robe. So you are punishing her?"

"Until I get back my robe and my chicken and my fifty-four cents she can stay here until she rots!"

"Tell me, Kalfu, has she not had enough punishment?"

"Never, never!"

"What kind of robe did you have?"

"A red robe. A red, rose-colored robe."

"What kind of chicken?"

"A Dominique chicken."

"If I see that the robe and the chicken and the fifty-four cents are returned, will you let her go?"

"I want what's mine," said "Kalfu."

"I'll see that you get the things."

"If you don't—mmhmm!"

"You needn't worry," said Reser. "I'll replace them."

"If that is the case," replied "Kalfu," "*bonsoir!*"

"*Bonsoir*," said Reser. With that Kalfu left, and the woman without a name fell quietly asleep.

In a few moments she awoke and leaped to her feet, crying out, "Where am I? What kind of place is this? I left home yesterday morning to go to Ti-Goâve . . ."

"You left home yesterday morning?" Reser interrupted. "You have been here for two years."

"What is this place?"

"Have you ever heard of Pont Beudet?"

"The crazy house? I am not crazy!"

"Kalfu tells me you tore up his robe."

"Kalfu!"

"He says you stole his chicken and you spent his fifty-four cents."

"I did, I did!" she cried.

"Why did you?"

"Because I had no luck with my life. I say, the devil with Kalfu. The devil with the *loa*. I'm going to be a Protestant!"

"Be a Protestant," Reser answered. "But before you do and before you will ever be happy anywhere, make your peace with Kalfu. I promised him that he would get a new robe, a red, rose-colored robe of silk. I promised him a Dominique chicken and fifty-four cents. You must give these things to him before you can have peace in your soul."

Quietly she said, "You will do all that for me—and for the *loa?*"

"I have told you what we will do," Reser replied. "By the way, what is your name?"

"Christiane."

"*Bonsoir,* Christiane, and sleep well."

Reser ordered a seamstress to make the robe for Kalfu. He got a chicken. He put aside fifty-four cents for Kalfu, Guardian of the Crossroads, one of the most truculent of the deities. Kalfu always demanded that which was his. When he threatened to leave Christiane in the asylum until she rotted he was not fooling.

Reser had all the required things ready and informed Christiane that he would send her home on Monday. Kalfu would not accept the offerings until they had been presented to him in his own *hounfort.* This, too, Reser did.

Then, on the following Sunday afternoon, the matron came hurrying into Reser's office. "*Docteur!*" she exclaimed. "Kalfu wants to see you!"

Reser went to Christiane's room, and Kalfu had again entered her head.

"You are sending her home tomorrow?" "Kalfu" asked.

"I am," Reser replied.

"That is Monday?"

"Monday."

"Wait one more day" was the command.

"Why?"

"Wait one more day!"

"Any reason?"

"Yes, good reason," said "Kalfu."

"What?"

"You will find out. Trust me."

"Kalfu" would say no more. Then he left Christiane, and she spoke to Reser. "Have you come to take me home?"

"Tuesday," said Reser.

"Tuesday? Why not Monday as you promised?"

"Tuesday," he repeated shortly.

On Tuesday morning Reser and a matron rode with Christiane to Port-au-Prince where she intended to get transportation to Ti-Goâve. They got to the city and were heading south on the Rue du Quai in congested traffic. They turned out of their lane and were forced to stop directly in the path of a truck heading north. The two vehicles halted bumper to bumper. As they did so a young man jumped out of the truck. Christiane caught sight of him, let out a scream of recognition and opened the car door. The young man seized her hand and drew her into his arms with a sob. "Christiane, my sister!" he cried. "We thought you were dead! Here you are alive and well!"

Reser looked upon the scene. He had to laugh at the shouts of the drivers who were honking their horns and asking what right he had to block the traffic. Right? Every right! The right of the *loa*. Kalfu had spoken and his will had been done.

3.

"YOU KNOW what I'd like to do?" I said to Reser one day after we had finished lunch in his cottage. "Run down to the old seaport town of Jacmel and see some of Haiti's south country."

He looked at me. "Say that again!"

"Jacmel on the southern coast."

"I thought I heard right. You got that idea right out of my mind."

"Don't tell me I'm getting that way!" I said with a laugh.

"Maybe you are," he retorted. "Nobody ever suggests going to Jacmel. But I was just thinking that we should go."

"I'll rent a *ligne*," I promised.

"To get to Jacmel we have to ford a river fifty-two times going down."

"And fifty-two times coming back?"

"That's not being psychic. Just logical," he replied. "What do you expect to find at Jacmel?"

"Something will turn up," I answered. "We'll take Lorena along. She can get some pictures—of us fording the stream a hundred and four times."

He weighed the suggestion a moment and said, "Agreed." I thought again what an odd picture he made as he sat in the small room with the drums leaning against the wall, the two black boys watching him with strange reverence, and near-by on a table altar a crucifix and several *pierre loa*. A Voodoo contemplative in his monastic cell! As he sat there with arms folded across his chest, the tattooed dragon beaming brightly and his eyes having the far-off "look of the *loa*" in them, I could understand why he had been called the white god of Voodoo-land. He looked upon life as he looked into the crystal ball or the glass of water, seeing things which others did not see.

"Is there Voodoo in Jacmel?" I asked.

"There is Voodoo everywhere in Haiti," he said.

"How about leaving at eight in the morning?"

"That's just what I was thinking," he reflected. Our eyes met.

"Walk down to Bizoton Road with me," I invited.

"I was just planning to."

On the bus back to town I went over some notes I had made. Underneath the yellow sheets were several letters. One was Paul Ramsey's almost forgotten warning—"Don't go to Haiti! Voodoo is snake worship and black magic!" This seemed ridiculous. Surely nothing unfortunate had happened and only good had come my way since arriving in Haiti. Voodoo, I was beginning to feel, might mean good luck. Strange the ideas which people like Ramsey had.

The melodic jargon around me drew me closer to the fascinating spell of the Enchanted Isle. I was beginning to understand a word here and there, sometimes a phrase. I was beginning to interpret the spontaneous laughter and the freedom of the Haitian peasant. Just now I felt that a few of Reser's beliefs had become mine—only a few, but those few were good. "His people" lived with companions unseen, but very near. The *loa* understood their struggles and their escapes. The *loa* guarded them jealously, asking only what was theirs, demanding justice, imparting joy.

I looked out over the Caribbean. It was Agué's. Agué guarded it. The cemetery was Guedé's. He knew all about the dead. The mountains and gardens belonged to Azaca Médé. The trees and shrubs to Loco. The open doors of the shops and homes were Legba's. The crossings were watched over by Kalfu. All was the *loa's* and the *loa,* as Reser so often said, worked best in Haiti.

I was pleased, though I did not quite know why, that he imagined I had picked the proposed trip to Jacmel out of his thoughts. I reflected that all of this meant I was beginning to understand the spirit of Voodoo. Perhaps I was, but nevertheless Lorena kept insisting that the native faith, like the country, could best be revealed through pictures.

She eagerly seconded the suggestion of going to Jacmel, because feminine intuition told her that if we got away from Reser's friends in the Port-au-Prince area, he would not be so opposed to the trip of the shutter. Surely he would not object to her taking pictures of strangers. Surely he had no superstition about the influence of the "little black box." Or had he?

When we were in the car and well on our way the matter of pictures came up, and Reser said, "I don't think you can disregard the beliefs of these people and get away with it."

"What do you mean?" Lorena asked.

"Oh," he said wisely, "the *loa* watch over their own."

He did not seem too serious. In fact, Lorena's mind was put at ease. She had thought in terms of native violence—someone breaking her prized Medalist, perhaps. She was willing to take her chance with the *loa!* Apparently she felt that the ubiquitous *mystère* would know that her intentions were honorable. The negatives she had developed in her wardrobe darkroom were of such good quality, they seemed to prove that the saints were on her side.

So all was well as we started a trip which, according to the map, looked like a drive of about a hundred kilometers—some sixty-two miles. The map was unnecessary. Reser knew every twist and turn of the way. A good stretch of road went as far as the picturesque village of Carrefour, twelve miles from Port-au-Prince. From there it was dust and stones as far as Grand-Goâve. Crowded *camions* raised up clouds of dirt and the walking people packed it down with their callused bare feet as they trudged eastward and westward singly and in groups.

Reser was so well acquainted with this section of Haiti that we played a game as we drove along. From time to time he told us how far we had come from Port-au-Prince. With unfailing skill he hit the correct mileage every time. Six miles, seven miles, eight, nine—Lorena would take her hand off the mileage indicator. Whatever the miles or the kilometers were, he guessed right.

"How do you do it?" we wanted to know.

"Landmarks," he explained. "I used to travel this road so much that I spotted telltale signs. Six miles was a rice paddy. Seven was *mer frappé* where the road comes close to the water of the bay. Eight, a cutaway between two banks. Nine, three lone coconut trees in a marsh. The royal palm looming up over there, that's a mileage sign for me. I know how far we are at that point as clearly as if the kilometers were blazed on the trunk."

He did not pretend to play this game after we turned south off the main road. Abruptly we found ourselves on an abandoned wagon road running along the shoulder of a mountain. It climbed and dipped and curved through heavily wooded gorges and past several hopefully cultivated terraces. We might have coped easily with the road had it stayed, as any decent road should, on dry land. This one soon became mostly river. Although I had been prepared for fifty-two crossings, it was quite another thing actually to be in the midst of them.

The two streams, the Gosseline and the Grande Riverie, which weave like a symbol of Damballa in and out of this rocky jaunt to Jacmel, are innocent enough in their initial invitation to the unwary driver. They let him see the solid graveled river basin through clear and shallow water. The first crossings are easy. They provide a sense of refreshment for the dusty car and cool comfort for the travelers. Then, after a dry and hazardous mountain climb, the descent leads to a series of fords that were never intended for anything on wheels. The road takes on the dizzy pattern of the river. It becomes a series of hairpin curves narrowly clawed out of the jungle, a group of half-moons alternating tip to tip and weaving back and forth across the streams.

Five, ten, twenty times we splashed through for a jostling baptism on this humid and darkening day. Then, on the twenty-second or twenty-fourth crossing, our "highway" suddenly ended. Reser said there would be places like this where we would have to drive not *over* the stream, but along *with* it in the channel. The river varied in width from ten to thirty feet at this point. The idea was to keep the car in shallow water and on solid footing. We maneuvered the first of these long stretches so successfully that Lorena tied up her skirt to wade out through knee-deep water and got the photographic evidence that our car was amphibious.

On the thirtieth crossing, more or less, things were different. The gravel crust on which we had been inching forward crackled and broke like a glass bowl. We started to sink. Water rushed over the floor boards.

"*Ai-yai-yai!*" was Reser's comment.

The motor spluttered and died, but the car settled firmly. We scrambled out with Lorena holding cameras high above her head. As we stood on the bank squeezing the water out of our clothes I remembered that we had not encountered a single other vehicle since leaving Grand-Goâve. We had not seen any other human beings for at least an hour. It looked like a long walk or an even longer wait. Lorena did not mind. She was already trying to persuade me to wade back and sit behind the wheel. It was then I remembered that the man from whom I had rented the *ligne* had warned me that floods in the valley were common and that mountain rains came suddenly and often daily to send the rivers into a roaring torrent. I looked apprehensively from the sky to Reser.

"What's the best plan?" I asked. "Is there a telephone within ten kilometers?"

"Not within fifty" was the answer. "But we'll get out."

"With a man-sized miracle we will," I answered dubiously.

"Well, we'll try the miracle," he said.

Cupping his hands around his lips, he let out the most primitive, earsplitting yell I have ever heard. Twice he shrieked his siren call, "OW-W-W-W-E-E-E-E-e-e-e!"

"What's that?" I asked. "A Voodoo SOS?"

He stood tensely. "Wait and see."

I glanced at Lorena. She was changing a film. She looked at me. That was about all the time that elapsed before the thick stalks in a sugar-cane field parted and a black face peered out. Then a hand with a machete pushed the cane aside farther.

"Bonjour!" said Reser.

"Bonjour!" White teeth showed in a broad smile as the black man stepped into the clearing. On the other side of the stream his counterpart appeared. Then next to this one another and another until eleven men had emerged from the thicket and stood casting amused glances from us to the half-submerged car.

Then the scene was broken by a cry, "Doc!" A black peasant, swinging his machete joyously over his head, sloshed across the stream.

"Ai-yai-yai!" said Reser and held out his arms to embrace the man.

To the accompaniment of emphatic gestures, fluent Creole began to flow, and the white man soon had his black brothers around him in a magic circle. He had them wrapped in laughter as he dramatized how the *ligne* had conspired to carry us all straight down to Agué's "island below the sea." Our predicament was changed suddenly into a spontaneous party worth more than the discomfort and soaking we had received. The business of getting the car to dry land was a labor of love accomplished by the wholesome joy of the game. Lorena got pictures to prove that it is possible for eleven stocky Haitians and two whites to carry a waterlogged Chevrolet thirty feet and then shake the Grande Riverie out of it!

Fortunately we had salvaged some bottles of kola and *clairin* and a package of sandwiches, all of which was in keeping with the mood of the occasion and cut down the passage of time while the coils dried out. It was a grand party while it lasted, a good interlude, rich in the kind of thing that makes the island a land of perpetual charm. The black men had no thought of getting back to work, nor was there concern about whether or not we ever got to Jacmel. The moments were spent for the moments' sake, and apparently everyone felt that the *loa* had planned it all that way.

Reser beat out drumbeats on the fender of the car and sang a few songs, including one for our erstwhile sick child, the automobile:

> *Pitite mué malade,*
> *'Mallé caille gangan Simbi-d'l'eau,*
> *Si li bon gangan*
> *Pitite mué sauvé;*
> *Nan misere um té; y-oh!*

My child is sick,
I go to the house of the *houngan,*
If he be a good priest
My child is saved;
I was in pain; y-oh!

He had a proverb that was apropos: *Leï' cabrouet ou collé ou connaï nom boefou.* (When your cart is stuck you know your oxen's names.) And a Haitian riddle: A pregnant woman comes to a river. The child jumps over. What is it? The answer, A loaded gun, put the men into ecstasy.

When we were ready to leave they ran alongside the car until we had crossed and recrossed the stream several times. After warm handclasps all around they stood and waved their good-bys until we were hidden from view.

Almost dubiously Lorena said, "I didn't know that you had friends here or that even the men in the sugar-cane swamps know you."

"I have friends everywhere," Reser replied confidently. "Once in north Haiti, far from a town, I was with a party going to Christophe's palace at Sans-Souci. All of a sudden a passer-by called out, 'Hey, Doc!' You can go the length and breadth of the island, and it won't be any different."

Lorena glanced at me and patted her camera consolingly.

"How about that Ow-w-e-e-e-e?" I asked.

"It's a summons," he said, "a way of rounding up friends. It may have looked mysterious, but that's Haiti. Walk a few hundred feet into the jungle or take off into a swamp, you're never alone. Climb the highest mountain and you'll find friends."

He wanted us to know that the affections of these people went deep, that they were shrewd observers, that their senses of perception had been sharpened by living close to the earth. Until they find out what a stranger is like, he explained, the natives play dumb. They are very cautious, very scrutinizing. Many visitors get them wrong, because they never get to know them.

For a full two hours, while we played hide and seek with the Gosseline, Reser talked about his adopted country and its people. Every crossing was exciting, for the river was running deep, and now at several fording points the black peasants had gathered to watch us as we cautiously picked our course. It seemed almost as though our rescuers had sent telepathic signals that we were coming, or perhaps their sharp sense of hearing had spotted the exasperating backfiring of our car. Women looked up from where they washed clothes on the rocks, and those who bathed in the crystal pools shouted at us that we were muddying up the water.

After the fifty-second crossing there was more of the same pock-marked road until the country began to spread out, and we struck the aged cobblestone streets of Jacmel. Reser was justified in saying, "When you see this town you see a Haitian city as it was centuries ago. Jacmel is Haiti unspoiled." He meant that the white man had not invaded it. We saw no *blancs*. There were no cars, no busses, no honking of horns. It was like dropping into an ancient Biblical village.

The soft-shaded, pastel-tinted houses were of French colonial design, faced with much iron-grill embroidery and gay overhanging porches. The homes were built along successively rising levels of the narrow streets and gave the appearance of standing almost one on top of the other, as if wanting to climb into the hazy sky; while southward, below and beyond, the level blue of the Caribbean stretched far out into the world away.

The worn old streets were lulled into the sleepy magic of mid-afternoon. The November sun burned down on seemingly deserted shops, but, as we drove by, dark-skinned proprietors appeared in them mysteriously. A gendarme eyed us with a glance of casual questioning, twirled his cocomacaque—his club—and sauntered away.

Jacmel unspoiled was Haiti undiscovered. Few tourists came here. They stayed in Port-au-Prince. They flew to Cap-Haïtien and to the Citadel of King Christophe, called the eighth wonder of the world. To me, Jacmel was the ninth wonder. Its miracle lay in the fact that no one had commercialized its fabulous beach or brought a rush of hungry artists to its tempting scenes. Now one photographer intruded. She got a picture of an irresistible subject, but only over Reser's objections. He had called our attention to it, however, with his sudden "Oh-o! Oh-o!"

A woman was striding down the street with arms swinging. A big cigar stuck out of her lips. Her head was wrapped around with a black turban. She was possessed. "Guedé," Reser pointed out. "Guedé has mounted her. It's Guedé all right!"

Lorena snapped the shutter.

"I wouldn't do that," Reser said, his tone one of caution with a slight show of irritation. He was always protecting the people, though he made it seem as if he were protecting us. Was he really superstitious? Did he really think something might happen to Lorena if she persisted in getting a picture story?

With our relations somewhat strained, we drove around to the hotel where a solitary car was parked. There would be no difficulty getting accommodations here. Apparently we were the only outsiders; so far as I knew we were the only whites in this town of 15,000. But no matter how many travelers there might have been, we would have received special treatment, for the manager greeted Reser like an old friend. We were hardly inside the cool, high-ceilinged rooms before refreshments were provided.

Doc was recognized wherever he went with the exception of a single instance. When he and I walked to the Jacmel market he had the experience of being, for a little while, a stranger in his adopted land.

We were going up a sloping street when we heard voices behind us. A group of Haitians were at our heels taunting us in Creole and repeating, *"Blanc—Blanc"* which I knew by now meant "You dirty white." Reser whispered to me, "Don't look around. Say nothing. Just keep walking."

We did, but the voices became more boisterous and insulting. The group was ganging up on us. Reser and I walked on, shoulder to shoulder.

"Do you know what they're saying?" I asked.

"Sure I know what they're saying," he grumbled. "You find packs like this in any city anywhere."

"What do you think? What's best to do?"

"Say nothing. Do nothing."

The gang was working alongside us, trying to get us to make a move against them. "Hi, *Blanc! Blanc!*"

Reser stopped and touched my arm so that I halted, too. We turned and faced the men. There were six of them, deep black, one of them very large and muscular with an ugly gash across his cheek. This one hurled one more insult at us, and then Reser quietly raised his hand. Without a show of excitement but with obvious emotion he spoke in his warmest and most musical Creole. *"Pouqui ou juré mué Blanc? Ce pas faute mué si Bon Dié té gagne temps bai ou tout coleur li avan li té fé mué?"*

A look of pain and sorrow crossed his face when he said that. The men looked at him, and their eyes grew large. The big man was the first to draw back in great astonishment. The others also retreated step by step as if withdrawing from some holy thing.

Reser nodded sadly as he looked at them, but he directed his words to me. "You see," he said, "they're not so bad."

"What was it you said?"

"I said, 'Why do you taunt me by calling me white? Can I help it if God ran out of color when he got 'round to making me?'"

4.

BUT FOR Reser I would never have seen family altars hidden behind secret shelves or concealed in cupboards or openly displayed in the humble rooms of many a Haitian home. But for him, I would never have knelt with peasant families and learned how deeply they believed in the *loa* or how much the faith meant to them in their search for meaning behind the experiences of life. In the Jacmel country his friends became mine, even to the proprietor of a small confectionery, a man who had once been an inmate at Pont Beudet. Reser had effected his cure through treatment based on an understanding of possession.

Always there was Voodoo. Not Voodoo as cannibalism and witchcraft, not Seabrook's Voodoo or St. John's Voodoo or Lindsay's "fat, black bucks," but Reser's Voodoo as the setting in which he had found his pearl of great price. As far as he was concerned, Catholicism held the official position as the state religion, but Voodoo held the people. It was coexistent with their customs, ideals and traditions. It carried out its mission in a manner peculiar to itself. The true religion of the island was the constant consciousness of the *loa's* presence. Why had writers never mentioned the fact that Voodoo was gentleness and faith and family songs? Or why weren't we seeing sex-mad orgies? Did these no longer exist? Or was Reser simply showing us what he wanted us to see?

"Bless the altar," he would say during our visits to Haitian homes. Then I would take the bottle of cologne or Florida water and sprinkle the cross, the *pierre loa* and the various bowls and dishes. I would stand for a moment and meditate on many things. The sign of the cross, the kissing of the beads, the chanting of the prayers always made me wonder where Mother Church left off and where Voodoo began, or where American Christianity stopped and African paganism took over.

One afternoon we sat in the manager's quarters in the hotel at Jacmel while Reser tested a Voodoo drum. He liked the deep resonant tone. Alternately bending over the drum and swinging his body back, he registered the cadence of the savage rhythm, and the blackness which God had not given him he created out of his own primitive passion. He hammered it out of the taut cowhide. A dozen, a hundred, a thousand times the sequences were repeated until the spell lodged in his soul, and the spirit of Cicéron overcame him. With the tips of his fingers and the heels of his hands he made the instrument speak, and the dragon on his arm was like Damballa dancing.

Even though he paused, the sound did not stop. Outside in the street drums were beating.

"*Ai-yai-yai!*" he cried in delight. "Listen to that. It's a crew coming from a *coumbite!*"

He led us out. On the other side of the street some thirty men were marching as though on their way to a celebration. Some of them, stripped to the waist, twirled their shirts as they paraded merrily on. A few brandished machetes. Three of the men had snare drums strapped to their bodies, and two others blew heartily on *vaccines,* the bamboo clarinets.

"How do you know they are coming from a *coumbite* and not going to one?" Lorena asked.

"Because of the hour. It's five o'clock. They've been working all day."

"They've been working all day and they feel like that?" she said with a laugh.

"That's what music does. At a *coumbite* the musicians are paid as much as the workmen."

"Is there any Voodoo connected with this?"

I asked the question because a *coumbite* had usually been referred to as a co-operative work project. Written accounts had compared it to a spontaneous help-your-neighbor project in the American Midwest where farmers pitch in and plow a field or harvest a crop or raise a house for someone who needs help. Reser said that in its deepest meaning the *coumbite* was a recognition of the brotherhood of man and the *loa's* concern for a people's need. He also called it entertainment and pleasure, but hidden within its mechanism he saw a Voodoo truth: rhythm generates a mystical force which lightens work. This, too, is the function of the *loa.*

He wanted us to see a *coumbite* in action. He wanted us to see it on a coffee plantation in the Morne La Hotte region, a land almost inaccessible, closed in by seven mountain ranges.

This meant retracing our course to the north coast, river crossings and all, and picking up National Highway 200. Passing west through Grand-Goâve and Petit-Goâve, we turned in a direction more west than south and recrossed this long, narrow, western-thrusting peninsula. We made our way through Fond de Negres to the Plain of Aquin and the old seaport town of Aquin some ninety kilometers from Grand-Goâve. Fifteen minutes from Aquin by car was the old fishing village of Zanglaise. Three mountains and five hours after leaving Zanglaise on muleback we started down into the most beautiful amphitheater in Haiti.

This mule trip took us through trails dotted by native shacks built out of the stuff of the earth, palm-thatched and primitive, surrounded by tobacco patches, flower gardens and banana trees and watched over by flocks of pigeons and birds with fabulous plumage and tropical tunes. Here one would have expected to find poisonous serpents and wild jungle animals. The black island has none of these. Haiti, as Reser so often said, has nothing to fear from within. As long as a man has a trail, a mule and faith, these will take him anywhere and never forsake him. But despite our possession of all three, the plantation was still five hard hours from civilization.

Everywhere in these hinterlands the land was rich in fruit and vegetables and medicinal herbs and plants. There were groves of sweet oranges, sour oranges and limes, great patches of citronella and dark-green rows of yams. Mahogany, mango, cedar and redwood trees stood like watchmen over the terraced plots of the unworldly peasants. Guinea grass, tall as a man on horseback, made us feel as though we were wading through seas of green. Rose apples abounded, and there was a saying that wherever the *pomme* rose grows the ground is kind.

Here as elsewhere we never got away from Reser's friends. We finally reconciled ourselves to the fact. The deeper we penetrated into the mountains the darker the people became. But even the blackest of them knew Reser or had heard of him. There was the girl who remembered how he had treated her when she was severely burned, and her mother who knew a strange English word—Barbasol.

"I had nothing with which to treat the girl's injuries," Reser explained, "nothing but Barbasol. I spread some of it on a leaf and put it over the girl's wound. It worked so well that the mother used to come to me with the leaf and ask for more of it. That's how she learned the word."

There was the man whom he had treated for boils, and there were people who remembered how he had fought yaws and intestinal diseases. There was much talk about herbs and magic, and there were always Voodoo and the altars. When would we get behind the scenes?

We saw the *coumbite,* and Lorena's camera worked overtime on that. Those who saw her said nothing. Reser said nothing. He was not incapable of seeing the photographic beauty of the *coumbite* "ballet." Here on the coffee plantation men, women and children picked the bright-red berries from branches which, in turn, seemed to have caught the sway of the music. The drummers were tireless mechanisms, and their rhythm robbed the workers of any fatigue. The men with the *vaccines* played with more enjoyment for their fellow workers than did entertainers in the night clubs of Port-au-Prince.

Suddenly a song leader raised his voice. As the toilers joined him they seemed to redouble their labors. I felt that I was hearing the work songs of the levees and the folk tunes of the cotton fields and the chants of the people to whom God had given color, until the music blended into a spiritual, half-Christian and half-Voodoo. The hands of the drummers moved faster, and the hands on the red-laden bushes caught the tempo. The branches swayed. Bursts of laughter punctuated the singing. The baskets and sacks filled magically. The burros and the burden-bearers kept step as they hauled their loads away.

Rhythm followed the coffee to the drying platforms where it was spread out and turned and rolled so that the great white *mystère,* the tropical sun, could change the cherry red into a shriveled gray husk within a few days. Rhythm accompanied it as it was put into the huge wooden mortars where two men with heavy, hardwood sticks stood on either side and with alternate strokes loosened the husks and poured the coffee berries out into huge piles. Now the women and girls working with their large, shallow, woven trays scooped up the coffee and tossed it into the air with a rhythmic motion. The wind carried the light husks away and the heavier ones were brushed aside with a deft motion of the hand. All of this was part of the ballet.

Coffee and rhythm. Voodoo and the altars. And the strange white man as their interpreter.

It rained here almost every evening. Whenever the clouds came down and covered the thatch-roofed houses with blankets of fog Reser only said, "Listen!" It was the signal for the beginning of a great natural orchestra as myriads of frogs began to sing in the swamps, and the lizards tuned in with their piercing musical whistle. Together they ran the scale from bass to treble with all the intervening notes. The air was filled with the fleeting lights of the innumerable *Kookooie,* fire-flies with running lights on their shoulders, large pairs of lights which flashed as large as a centime. At the edge of the mountain hung a deep ravine, and after rain had been falling a short time we could hear the roar of the water rushing down to the accompaniment of the Voodoo drum Reser played. On such nights the sky was black, but when the weather cleared the stars were brilliant lights so close overhead that, seemingly, a man with a good reach could turn them on or off.

Clear nights were storytelling time around the open fire. The smell of the moist earth, the persistent fragrance of gardenias and the scent of the pitch-pine smoke drifted in and out of this Eden. The black figures owning nothing yet owning everything were to Reser God's first created beings. Their white teeth and flashing eyes were the bright jewels with which the *Gran Mait* had adorned them. The magnificently formed bodies were His image. These secluded creatures of the Enchanted Isle had never tasted of the tree of the knowledge of good and evil. Reser maintained that they had few inhibitions. Their sensitive natures could blow up into quick anger like a summer storm and, like the storm, soon pass. Their moods were like the elements, but their words and their lives were part of the land, and the land was good.

Someday I would have to ask Reser to translate the repertory of stories joyously exchanged around the warming flames—stories that began with the narrator saying, *"Cric!"* and the listeners responding, *"Crac!"* These were signals that speaker and audience were ready. Favorites were the tales of Bouki and Ti Malice, Haiti's leprechauns—stories known throughout the country, and no other white man knew them better than our friend Doc.

All this was an interesting insight into Haitian peasant life. But I was impatient and said to Reser one day, "There must be a Voodoo service somewhere soon."

"Why?" he asked.

It was a good question. I could have answered by saying, "I
hope so." I said instead, "I just have a feeling there ought to be
one."

"You're right," he replied. "I have just been told there is to
be a dedication of a new *hounfort,* a Voodoo chapel, near Port-
au-Prince. We're going."

In prospect of this, he asked one of the women to prepare a
fitting toast—coffee!

Lorena got the sequence in color as the woman roasted the
beans in an iron kettle in which had been placed some coarse
brown sugar called *rapadeu.* When the coffee was a deep sepia
she ground it in a mortar, poured boiling water over it, let it
stand for a few moments and then filtered it through a muslin
bag.

Reser poured the aromatic ebony fluid into tiny cups, and we
drank to the *hounfort* and the service to be. He smacked his
lips in sheer delight. "This," he exclaimed, "is the drink of the
gods. Isn't it terrific?"

"I've often wondered," I said skeptically, "just what Haitian
coffee must taste like in order to be good."

"Like this!" he exclaimed. "Black as night, sweet as sugar
and hot as hell!"

Lorena and I were forced to agree that this was it.

5.

WE HAD driven hard and long back through
the peninsula country and were ready for the luxury of city
conveniences in Port-au-Prince. Reser informed us there was
no time for even a thought of this. It was late afternoon and

nearing the hour for the dedication of the *hounfort*. There was still a mountainous drive ahead, and he was insisting that we be on time. An air of unusual seriousness hung over him. In fact, we all had a feeling of something solemn impending. It had been a day in which we encountered a certain difficulty in a meeting of minds, a sunless day with occasional spatterings of rain, and with Reser as imperious as the heavy sky.

It may have been that the things we talked about along the way had plunged us into a tangle of opinions. We again discussed the relationship of the Catholic Church to Voodoo. I remarked that I had met a priest who said he wanted to see Voodoo rooted out and claimed there was no connection between Voodoo and Mother Church. Reser settled that with a note of exasperation. "He means there is no more connection than there is between New York and Manhattan!"

We also talked about psychical demonstrations, Lorena frankly admitting that she attributed such things to coincidence and chance.

As if to assure us that in his case it was the operation of a supernormal force Reser said, "There was once a German fellow who talked like that. He said to me, 'This business of anybody knowing anything about such things is bosh.' I asked him, 'Do you know an Adolph?' 'I know hundreds of them,' he said. I told him that this was a particular one, and he asked me to describe him. 'I see him in a bakery,' I said. 'I get the odor of cinnamon buns. I see him smoking a long pipe with a metallic cover. I see a woman near him. She is small and slender. Her hair is black, parted in the middle and tied into a knot at the back.' 'That's my wife you are talking about,' cried the German. 'That's my uncle who is the baker and who is smoking the pipe!' 'I see a girl dressed in blue and white. She is singing in a vested choir.' 'That's my sister!' 'I see a man badly burned lying in an engine room. He tried to shut off a valve on a broken steampipe.' 'That happened to my brother-in-law!' the German burst out. 'But who are you? Jesus Christ?' Don't tell me that was all coincidence!"

Everything in the way of conversation had been wrong. Lorena had called our attention to a goat hobble-tied in a peasant's yard. She observed that she had seen many evidences of Haitians' cruelty to animals. She mentioned pigs with long, heavy yokes which prevented them from pushing their heads through fences or thickets, turkeys and ducks tied by their legs and fastened to boards, chickens strung upside down and slung carelessly over the shoulders of the vendors, burros loaded with packs of charcoal, bananas and water-filled calabashes until their bodies sagged.

"Why do they treat their animals like that?" she complained.

Reser shrugged, and I said jokingly, "Maybe the peasants believe in reincarnation. Maybe they think that the spirits of the French and Spanish taskmasters who persecuted them are now in those animals. This might be their way of getting even."

"I wouldn't say that," Reser spoke up. "I'd rather say they aren't cruel in the first place, because they *aren't*. Some of the things are matters of expediency. If Haitians came to the States, they'd be shocked at some of your customs. I wonder what they would say about the mass murder of animals in your overloaded trucks or the open branding of cattle or vivisection or even the way chickens are crated. Deep in their hearts, black people are less callous and more gentle than whites."

He saw in these people what we did not see. We bemoaned their poverty—the per-capita income is forty dollars a year. He saw the spiritual riches of their unconcern about money. We felt their need for education—eighty per cent are illiterate—but he said, "I want to be sure what you mean by education. Most Haitians have an intuitive sense that serves them better than a formally trained mind. My houseboys can go to the market without a written list. They come back and tell me exactly what everything cost. They have great native intelligence. All over the island I can show you examples of phenomenal minds. Mathematical, philosophical and artistic geniuses are part of the tradition."

He honestly felt that, without luxuries, the Haitian still knew how to enjoy life better than did most Americans. Practically no peasant owned a car, radio or refrigerator, but he was contented. He was better adjusted than the people who set these things as their goals. He was better integrated mentally. Without modern implements the Haitian farmer worked his tiny plot of land and had no fear of being trammeled by the force of competition.

What he was saying was that we ought to understand once and for all that he knew, loved and respected these people. Long ago he had taken his stand as the champion of their cause and defender of their faith. These facts he made clear to us, particularly on this day when he was doing us the honor of opening the *hounfort* doors. I suppose he felt that he was taking a chance every time he trusted a white man to understand his motives. Perhaps much of what I interpreted as impatience was merely his deep-seated wish that I, too, might turn out to be a different kind of *blanc*. For, surely, if I sometimes caught the thoughts which floated in his mind, I must know that he bore within himself the guilt of those whites who had inflicted shocking cruelties upon the ancestors of Haiti's millions. For their reckless torture he wanted to make amends. For their sins he wanted somehow to be a redeemer.

He directed us to the dead end of a precariously worn-out road. Here we parked the car and started walking along a rocky slope that led upward between thatch-roofed huts and across open yards. At intervals a path had been machete-cleared through clumps of thicket, and here we could see that the earth had been tamped down by many feet. Lorena, trudging just ahead of me, hopefully lugging a camera and flash equipment, seemed very tired. Reser, in the lead, sang no song to cheer us on the way to this early evening service.

I watched his swinging stride. It was the walk of the hill people marked by easy grace, fully relaxed, tireless in its motion. This was no affectation. It was his natural instinct. He strode through this *hounfort* trail as he walked anywhere in Haiti, a symbol of confidence and honesty with himself. Whatever we might think about Voodoo made no difference to him at this moment. Whatever anyone thought about it or had written about it was irrelevant. If at one time it had been cannibalism or snake worship, mysticism or black magic, these things, if they ever existed in even the slightest degree, had merely been part of its fight for freedom so that it might emerge into a meaningful religious concept. Reser would probably have said that every faith once had its derelictions and that even Christianity had its massacres, its inquisitions and its holy wars.

He paused at the top of the trail and beckoned us to his side. With a motion of his hand, as if unveiling a Voodoo mural, he directed our interest to the scene in the *hounfort* yard. It was idyllic. People and country blended into a similitude of worship which might have been a rural churchyard on a Sabbath evening. The *hounfort* was a rectangular, gray adobelike structure without a steeple. It was guarded by the purple-gray mountains which the sky was just beginning to tint with broad brush strokes of flamingo red. All around the cleared patches of turf was the variegated vegetation of the tropics, fan palms and ferns, great clusters of exotically flowering shrubs, giant flowered stalks of red poinsettias.

The spotlessly white-clad *hounsi,* whose faces and limbs shone radiant black, dotted the grounds. A group of men dressed in white and a large assemblage of women, some in white, others in colorful print dresses, moved about. Most of the women wore the broad-brimmed hats of the peasants, a few had donned head scarves and all were barefooted. The sight of neatly dressed children, silk Voodoo flags, a tethered burro and the general scene provided a picture so striking that Lorena could not resist bringing it into focus. Reser glanced at her but said nothing.

We stood together under the spell of the kind of Voodoo he wanted us to see, a dignified, seemingly well-planned gathering with the *mambo* now emerging through the *hounfort* door.

Her attention was called to our presence. She looked up. Her teeth flashed white in a happy smile of recognition as she saw Reser. With a few hasty orders to her male assistant she came to meet us as we started down.

She halted for just a moment, a dramatic studied pause, during which she took Lorena and me into account. Then her eyes shone bright as she got from Reser a reassuring glance and warm words of greeting prefaced with his characteristic "Oh-o!

Oh-o!" In this case the expression could have been one of admiration. She was slender and lithe and perilously pretty. A red turban wrapped smartly about her head, a white dress, tied around with a colorful sash, comprised a ceremonial attire of simple beauty. Rare sensitivity was here, and an aliveness to every sound and impression was registered in her movements. The mystical signs, the words that passed between her and Reser were marked with piety and hinted of secret joy. When she shook hands with us she laughingly crossed her wrists, indicated that we should do the same, and then shook hands with us three times with a violent downward motion. Talking animatedly to Reser, she escorted us to where the people were waiting. Again we were drawn into the circle, impressed and pondering upon the unconcealed harmony that existed between the white man and his Voodoo friends. The affection transcended color and culture. It went beyond these into a mysterious faith, and I wondered whether the open *hounfort* door might be the omen that we, too, might be able to enter it.

We were given choice seats in the *hounfort* yard in a row of chairs facing the drummers. Unhurriedly others found places and the children selected spots on the ground where they could watch the ceremony. The preliminaries proved again that nothing is ever hurried at a Voodoo service. The *loa* are timeless. It was an occasion for an exchange of news about people and events and also a period for a close inspection of the exterior of the *hounfort*. The gray, rectangular, wattled "temple" was about eighteen by forty feet in size and not over twelve feet high. It reminded me of the *morada* of the Penitentes in the American Southwest. Like these adobe chapels of the "self-crucifiers," the *hounfort* had the same stark, defensive appear-

ance and windowless walls. The door stood open. Painted on
the inside door panel was a series of symbols, emblems of the
gods, including the snake. The interior looked like a dark,
barren chamber, but we had been assured by Reser that every
hounfort consisted of two or three rooms with as many altars.
In the center of the main room, called the *bagui,* stood the chief
altar with its numerous articles and ritual paraphernalia.

Just now we were more concerned with the people. Everything about them bespoke solemn interest. Lorena's fingers
were itching to get this down in black and white, but already
the *loa* were drawing down the early evening shadows to thwart
her. The reefs of pink and deep blue on the mountains changed
to gray. Gently the shadows began to embrace the *hounfort*
and enfold the people. Perhaps this timing had been planned
to lend mystery to the affair and to make us conscious of our
union with the forces of nature on this lovely night. All in all
there was an inspiration here which I had not felt at any previous service.

Now the vivacious *mambo* picked up the *asson.* This ritual
rattle was to her as holy as a cross. It was like a magic wand
with which she cast a spell over us and transformed herself
into a priestess whose supple movements set the gods of earth
and sky in motion. A flash of a smile, bold and rapturous,
started the seductive roll of the drums and the mechanical clang
of the *ogan.* In a moment she was lost in the ecstasy of the *loa,*
and every motion to her was joy.

This was Voodoo lifted out of primitivism into a subjective
experience. The invocation to Legba was liturgy of a higher
order than we had heard in the peristyle. The chants and the
litanies had great dignity. For the first time I realized that the

drums served another function besides generating a hypnotic power. They were a musical accompaniment, much as an organ fulfills its function in formal services. This ceremony was definitely "high church."

I passed on to Reser some of my impressions. He shrugged as if to say that I should have recognized this quality in Voodoo long ago. But even he watched with almost breathless attention when the long column of white-clad, candle-bearing *hounsi* came from behind the *hounfort* and marched in striking silhouette against the southern sky. Carried in procession were the silk flags and articles for the *hounfort* altars.

Once more in turn the gods were invoked. Legba, Loco Atissou, Aizan Velakété, Damballa and Aida Ouedo, Sobo Bodare, Agasu, Agoné, Bossu Agaou, and Azaca, Ogan Balindo and Batala. A few lanterns were lighted. One, held high in the hands of the *mambo's* assistant, illumined a spot near the southeast corner of the yard. While the *hounsi* and the flag-bearers stood at attention an acolyte brought the bowl of meal, and the *mambo* proceeded to draw a *veve* on the ground. Out of the corner of my eye I saw Lorena stealthily press a flash bulb into the reflector. Frankly I, too, wanted this picture. I wanted it badly. To describe the making of a *veve,* one photograph would be worth a thousand words. The intricacies, the hovering hand, the flow of the white meal, the symbolism could all be captured with one quick trip of the shutter. Against this desire rose the strong opposition which I felt in the man who sat shoulder to shoulder with me. He said nothing. I doubted whether he saw Lorena's sly preparations, but I dreaded to arouse his displeasure. After all, we were only now getting started in our Voodoo research. We were still on probation! I nudged Lorena and shook my head, but she was not to be so easily dissuaded. She leaned forward, touched Reser lightly and asked with a glance if she had his permission. He answered with a glance that she did not.

The *veve* grew. The people watched with slavish attention. The *mambo's* attitude was one of poignant pleasure. Each time she dipped her hand into the bowl a smile, vivid and conquering, accompanied the act. The circle in which she worked became charged with a force from which we could not turn our eyes. Her ease of uninterrupted motion beguiled us. Her subtle murmur of satisfaction as she worked engrossed us in her magic. Her motions were hypnotic. A turning movement, the lift of a hand, the flow of the meal lured Lorena's attention from her camera. Together we waited the climax of the *veve* when the worshipers would read its meaning and register their acclaim.

At my side the white man watched and chanted to himself under his breath. I bent closer but could not catch his words. They sounded like a ritual prayer. Apparently he was reciting something which seemed to build the *mambo's* ecstasy, though she could not possibly have heard what he was saying. Yet frequently she glanced at him as if she understood.

Then, blending with the completion of the *veve,* timed as if to force us to hold our applause and turn our attention from the corn-meal drawing, a young man came from behind the *hounfort.* It was *la place* and he bore in his hands a chicken, a red cock, brilliantly preened. Its feathers glistened. Its colors were translucent. It rested in the acolyte's black hands, a precious sacrifice. All eyes were upon it, but none more watchfully than mine, for there was something about this chicken that bore the stamp of the *loa's* influence. It was not held by the outstretched hands of *la place;* it simply rested there with no sug-

gestion that it wanted to escape or that it would if it could—
and it could not. It was riveted to the imploring hands by some
devilish or holy power, I knew not which.

My first impression was that it was hypnotized—hypnotized
or drugged. Its body pulsed with the rise and fall of agonized
breathing. Its neck was thrust out. Its beak was open as if it
were burning with thirst.

Close by stood the *mambo*. Her breast rose and fell with the
panting of the captive bird. Her features wore a look of sensu-
ous longing, as if it were her spirit that was confined and caught
and ready to be offered up. Already I imagined her drinking
the warm blood as if it were a holy eucharist.

I could feel the telekinetic force that caused *la place* to fall
suddenly to his knees. His arms stayed outstretched, and in his
uplifted hands the chicken remained immobile, crouched and
terror-stricken as before.

The exotic servant of the gods raised her *asson* and made a
mystical sign in the open air. The shock of the drums intruded
with a dull throb, like dragons grumbling for their sacrifice.
A very black man stepped into the clearing with a piece of iron
that appeared to be a broken spade, got down on his knees and
started to dig at the stubborn earth. With the iron and his
clawing hands he grubbed out a hole while a chant rose like the
beating wings of the *mystère*.

The nocturnal magic deepened. From the mountains, standing like stage cutouts in silhouette, the drums and the singing
were flung back. In the canyons the sound was taken up by
nature's echoing cry. Close overhead the heavens declared the
glory of Voodoo by bringing out processions of stars, faint and
flickering as the candles burning in the *hounsi's* hands.

A secret voice told me that something momentous was about

to happen. It was a feeling prompted by the threefold scene: *la place* kneeling like a piece of sculptured mahogany offering up the agonized cock with its outstretched neck and lowered wings; the beautifully poised figure of the white-clad *mambo,* her body warmly embracing the throb of the drums; and the intensely black man clearing out the hole he had dug as solemnly as if he were digging a grave.

It was a grave. But only for a chicken, a chicken for Ogoun. Why should this moment be so tense, so charged with explosive force? Why did the scene seem cloaked in silence despite the pounding of the drums and the voices crying? It was the fact that the chicken was alive, yet not alive. It was alive, but powerless to resist. It was a symbol. A symbol of what? Of all that is fateful and predestined? Of all the heaped-up superstition that claims us all? It was something more. It was a symbol of one lone creature meeting God without the cushioning shock of death, forced to face the great Unknown alive and seeing. It was only a chicken, but when the *mambo* took it in her hands and blessed it it became a living soul.

She did not kill it. She could not. Ogoun wanted it alive. Did the earth cry out in anguish, pleading that for once it might receive a breathing thing, a thing whose heart was beating and whose blood was warm?

The man whose skin was darker than night moved aside. With infinite compassion the *mambo* placed the chicken in its cool and shallow grave. Breathlessly she withdrew her hands, gently as if she had just laid her first-born into its manger bed. Who would ever forget the silent power of those slender hands? From them some psychic power flowed to hold the feathered sacrifice against its will. From them a radiance fell to fill the sacrificial crypt with an uncertain light.

She gave a signal to the very black man, and he crept forward. In a moment his large outstretched hands began sweeping the dirt back into the hole. It fell upon the chicken's crimson wings and sifted around the outstretched neck. The bird made no sound, it uttered no cry, though it must have known it was being buried alive. The stunning force of a magical presence held it in its unseen grip. The *mambo* stood over the spot, a paradox of holy piety and fleshly passion. She watched the dirt pile layer by layer until it all became once more the *houn-fort* yard. Her face wore an expression of great achievement. She held in her presence the fearful climax of some mighty expiation. Not only Reser felt the rapture of it. We all felt it: Lorena and I, the people, the children. Our wills and our volitions were buried with the sacrifice.

I realized suddenly that the drums had stopped. The chanting had stopped. The yard and the mountains were still, deathly still. While the hands had covered the sacrifice the black hands of night had covered us.

The acolyte with the white bowl approached the sacred burial pit while the man smoothed the ground in place with servile hands. The *mambo* watched him as he gave the spot a final caressing pat. Then she dipped her right hand into the bowl and stooped over the place where the chicken lay. The meal fell from her hands like magic potions. Who knew what to expect? Who knew what would happen? Perhaps the sprinkling of the meal would work a resurrection of the sacrifice. Perhaps the ground would break, and Ogoun himself would rise!

The *mambo* made a faultlessly straight line, then a perfect circle, then a cross, followed by a series of interlacing lines. And then it happened. There was a blinding flash of light, a gasp from the crowd, an impulsive movement, a sudden stir and turning of the people toward us. Lorena had taken a flashlight picture.

I felt time and space falling away. The white man at my side had become a stranger. I not only read his mind, I felt his thoughts. He had been betrayed. We had betrayed him. We had exposed him falsely to his people. We had defiled the sanctuary of his faith.

It all happened in a swift moment, but it was recorded in an eternity of feeling. The eyes of the people were upon us, and a thousand additional eyes seemed to glare out from the dense black foliage. I could feel the hands of the people reaching out, and it seemed that unseen hands were there to help them. But Lorena was deliberately turning the film, and when I saw her doing that I realized that the *mambo* had never stopped in her drawing of the *veve*. Her face showed supreme control; her actions, superior grace. Her expression said, "This has been done against my will, against Doc's will. But it is done."

The moment passed. Lorena clamped her camera into its case and put the flash equipment away as if to assure us that this would not happen again. Slowly the people settled back, *la place,* the *hounsi* and the very black man turned their eyes away.

Reser gazed with tired eyes at me, and I felt that he was looking at me for the last time. There was a gulf between us, a fixed gulf, deep and wide. I was a *blanc.* An ordinary *blanc.* He shook his head as if telling himself that he should have known. A surge of understanding and sadness swept over me as he turned away to fix his eyes on the fresh earth as if his spirit, too, were buried there.

The streams of meal were falling, and the *veve* grew.

Chapter 4

I.

AFTER THE *HOUNFORT* DEDICA-
tion, when we had taken Reser to the gates of the Chez Pauline,
we all stood awhile as if debating what words should be said.
Lorena apologized for taking the picture, but that did not undo
what had been done, nor was it any guarantee that it would not
happen again. We were all dead tired. Halfheartedly we exchanged indefinite promises that we would see each other when
we were rested up, and so we parted.

The thought passed through my mind as we walked back to
the car that we might never see Reser again. With it came a
stubborn conclusion that he was altogether too close to the black
people to allow us the freedom we needed for our research.
There must surely be some other way to get the contemporary
story of Voodoo, and there must certainly be some acceptable
system by which Lorena could get her documentary.

We had learned a little Creole by hearing it so much. We
had a certain feeling for the land. And, as for the people, we
secretly believed that they would be willing to co-operate with
us if we only knew where and when the services would be held.
Although the Voodoo faith observed the important days of the

Christian year, it also followed a most unpredictable schedule. One might reasonably expect a meeting on Wednesday, Saturday and Sunday nights, but there was no actual assurance of it. There might be impromptu gatherings any time of the day or night and anywhere in the city or out of it. They occurred whenever the *loa* dictated—at whatever hour the priest or priestess deemed expedient. Lorena and I boldly decided to sally forth on our own.

I immediately ran into what I considered exceptionally good luck. Two days after the *hounfort* affair I met a woman of Jamaica in her sisal shop on the Rue F. Bathier. Our conversation got around to Voodoo, and when she spoke of it a vast vagueness came into her dark eyes.

"I have read of you in *Le Matin,*" she mused. "The news story said you are interested in this religion of Haiti. I have wanted to meet you."

"Are you a *mambo?*" I asked.

She nodded solemnly. "I can show you things you have never seen." Her voice was far off. "Voodoo heals. Voodoo reveals." Her lean brown hands tugged nervously at her worn leather purse. "Come to my home tonight. Come and see."

I was at the address on Lafleur Duchene at nine o'clock. A somewhat dilapidated two-story house stood darkly within the trees. The iron picket fence around the somber yard was broken down. The small gate hung half-open as though the place had long been unvisited. I followed the uncertain stone path to the porch, where a sheen of light outlined a curtained window. My rap at the door echoed through the rooms inside.

An elderly woman greeted me with a cordial *"Bonsoir"* and invited me in. Two spacious rooms were connected by an open archway, and here a group of Haitians sat solemnly in a semi-circle. I counted seven women and five men. Their eyes, sparkling white in the light of candles, lingered upon me as I was escorted to my place. No one spoke. The men on each side of me nodded as I greeted them. Their attention was fixed on the Jamaican woman who stood behind a large table on which candles were set amidst a collection of bowls and earthen jars.

She wore a red turban bound tightly around her head making her brown, lean face sharply featured and striking. Her eyes looked beyond us, and as I grew accustomed to the want of light I saw defiant strength in them.

"I have explained," she said to me in English, as if I were somewhere far away, "that I invited you. I have said that I hope the *loa* will have a message for you." I thanked her.

She made several signs with both hands over the candles and mumbled to herself. We watched and waited. Her face became suddenly tense, and she scowled, gazing fixedly into space. She shut her eyes as if to drive us out of her thoughts. Her body quivered, then trembled convulsively as if to throw off an unwanted possession.

In a moment she emitted a cry that rattled the windows and sent a tremor through the group. Her eyes flashed open. Her features changed to those of a person very old, her body began a weaving motion, starting at the hips and moving upward until her head snapped like a whip. This was repeated several times, and finally a broad grin formed on her lips. Nodding as if satisfied that her transformation was complete, she picked up a big cigar from the table and lighted it, using one of the sacred candles. She puffed energetically.

In a semientranced state she went from chair to chair giving lengthy messages in Creole. Sometimes she pirouetted a few times, and occasionally the twisting serpentine movement from trunk to head was repeated. After this she flipped the ashes from her cigar with a grand gesture, then planted herself in front of someone in the circle to give another "reading."

After a long hour of this, in which the individuals in turn agreed with her about the correctness of her prophecies and statements, she came abruptly over to me. With a glazed stare fixed upon me and the cigar pointed straight at me she said, "Your dog is all right!"

This brought me up with a shock. During the past few moments I had let my mind wander. I had just been thinking about our wire-haired terrier which had been left with friends back in the States. The *"mambo"* had picked the thought out of my mind with dramatic timing. I said, "Thank you very much."

"He's all right," she repeated and then grumbled as if arguing against an inner voice. She shook her head abjectly a few times, drew deeply at the cigar and accosted me with, "Who is Jimmie?"

"If it's the Jimmie I'm thinking of . . ." I began.

"It is!" she snapped. "You had trouble with him."

"That's right."

"About money."

"Yes."

"Wages."

"Wages."

"He worked for you on a house."

"On a cabin."

"A cabin is a house."

"All right."

"You will hear from him."

"Will I?" I asked doubtfully.

"I said you will hear from him!" she repeated, annoyed. "You will hear from him this week."

"Thank you."

She moved to the man next to me and proceeded to give him a message in Creole. For some thirty minutes more the clairaudient demonstration moved around the circle. It was all very serious. There was no laughter or humorous bantering such as one usually encounters in a spiritualistic circle, no asides to spirit controls, no begging of the question. Whatever she said was sharp, direct, positive. Only when she came out of her possessed state did her face relax. Only after another violent circular movement of her body and a snap of her head did she become once more the businesswoman whom I had met in the sisal shop.

As the circle broke up she extended her hand and thanked me for coming.

"Did you get a message?" she asked.

"Yes, I did," I told her. "Do you remember anything you said to me?"

"My dear sir," she said with a broad smile, "I remember nothing. Nothing at all. But let me know, won't you, if anything that was said has meaning? I have many wonderful things in store for you. I am called to many islands in the archipelago for services. Perhaps you would like to go along?"

About this, I told her, I would have to see.

Back at the Hotel Excelsior I gave Lorena an account of the séance.

She said, "We will never hear from Jimmie, Voodoo or no Voodoo."

Yet three days later we stood at the general-delivery window at *la poste* in Port-au-Prince and were handed an airmail letter from Jimmie mailed from Edmonton, Alberta, Canada.

Naturally this sent me back to the house on Lafleur Duchene for a series of private meetings. I was always mystified. The *"mambo"* usually stood before a Voodoo altar which held a crucifix, flowers and sweet-oil lamps with floating wicks. I sat near by. Sometimes there were chants and prayers and always there was the entranced state in which some foreign personality apparently pervaded the demonstrator. I had no idea where all this was leading me, but one thing was certain. She was getting across to me under the guise of Voodoo many things she wanted me to know and a few things she wanted me to do!

"Tell my horse," said the *"loa"* speaking through her on one occasion, "that you will help her publish a book. Tell my horse that you will help her arrange a series of meetings in the United States."

At this point my own *"loa"* was whispering to me not to do anything rash!

2.

IN A *tonnelle* not far from the village of Croix des Missions, Lorena attached a flash gun to her camera and plugged in an extension. It was early evening. A Haitian *mambo,* a very genuine one, and an assistant had gone out to get the corn-meal bowl and to dress in their ritual garments for the making of a *veve.* It was Lorena's big moment. Single-handed, with her *"Quitte um tiré portré ou, no?"* and a few additional phrases, she had persuaded this woman to allow her to take a series of pictures. A ten-dollar bribe had also helped.

This was not an actual service. The *tonnelle* was deserted, but the altar around the center pole held its customary furnishings, and the candles burned steadily in the necks of bottles. The *asson* or ritual rattle was prominently displayed. Three drums were suspended from a rafter as they are hung customarily when not in use. What we had not been able to do because of Reser's shielding of the people Lorena had achieved and she was glad. I had come along to hold the flash extension.

The *mambo* entered. She was well-fed, tall, and her large face was wreathed in a smile so broad that the ends of her mouth seemed to extend almost to the round golden earrings that dangled from beneath her red polka-dot turban. A white sleeveless dress fitted neatly over her heavy body. A red sash encircled her waist. Her acolyte was a lovely girl in her teens, dressed for the occasion in a gingham skirt and a white blouse over which hung luxuriant strands of *hounsi* beads. She bore the white bowl proudly in her shapely black hands.

Lorena was in her glory. For once she had time to arrange her subjects and compose her scene. For once she had co-operation, permission and a highly dramatic setting without a cluttering of spectators. She requested the *mambo* to start the *veve* so that a general outline could be seen.

"Soyez naturel," Lorena instructed, adding to the injunction of being natural that she wanted it to appear that this picture was being made at an actual service.

"Bon, bon," agreed the *mambo*. With this expression of "Good, good," Lorena focused on the flowing white meal.

Then she got the *hounsi* into just the right position and me

into the proper relationship with my extension reflector held as
high as my arm could reach. Carefully Lorena checked subjects
and equipment and double checked everything for a low angle
shot.

"*Soyez naturel*," she again cautioned the *mambo,* and in a
moment I heard the click of the shutter.

Nothing happened either to the flash gun or to the extension
which I held. There was not the faintest show of light.

Lorena said, "Now what?" She carefully went over the bulbs
and the connections. Then she tried it again. Blank darkness.
This time she said, "Well, now, what in the world!"

She put in new bulbs, minutely examined and reinserted the
connections, and again I stuck up my arm with the reflector at
the degree appointed. Again I heard the fateful sound of
the shutter. Simultaneously I also heard Lorena's exasperated,
"Well, I'll be damned!"

The *mambo* looked up. Her broad smile showed that she
was having the best time of any of us.

"*Lahn pan?*" she asked. This, I supposed, was her way of saying, "Something wrong?" I responded by saying there was something *cassé,* broken.

For a moment her eyes had a solicitous look, then a smile
showed glistening white teeth, and she hummed a little song
as she gracefully traced lines of meal to enlarge the *veve.* Lorena
took camera and flash equipment over to the altar and knelt
down in front of the candles.

The *mambo* giggled and said something to her assistant
which I could not understand. I surmised she was saying that
it looked as if the white woman was invoking the help of the
loa.

This white woman was doing no such thing. She was tearing the equipment apart and muttering, "This is the strangest thing I've ever seen." Her tone was hardly one of supplication. She asked me to bring her the flashlight from the car, which I did, and together we bent over the circle of light to find the trouble. I was sure I had found it. The bulbs simply needed a bit of burnishing where they made contact, a simple matter which I quickly rectified with a fingernail file.

"I hope you're right," said Lorena, "and it must be that, because I have never had this happen before."

Back we went to our positions.

"*Enco?*" asked the *mambo* pleasantly. That meant, "Again?"

"*Enco,*" said Lorena. "We are ready at last. *Soyez naturel.*"

"*Bon, bon,*" replied the *mambo*.

Maybe, I thought, it was all for the best, for as I got into my Statue-of-Liberty pose I realized that the *veve* had reached beautiful proportions. It represented a ship with streamers and flags and was really a work of art. Merrily the *mambo* was drawing shellfish into the sails while the assistant watched wonderingly over her bowl.

Lorena got set. Just for luck she tried a high angle shot this time and instructed me to change my position. I complied, thinking again what a rare opportunity this was, how mysterious the setting and the mood and how peaceful and far from the world these surroundings were. One could almost hear the falling of the meal and the flicker of the candles, it was so silent.

The snap of the camera was a loud report, and Lorena's disgusted outburst was like a pistol shot. "Has the devil gotten into this thing?" she sputtered.

She did not mean it just that way. She was too realistic for that. But I thought about it and was tempted to say that maybe it was exactly that—the devil had gotten into the flash equipment—the *Bakulu*, the evil one had gotten into it. Witchcraft and black magic were jamming the mechanisms!

Lorena was scolding herself. "All I brought was this one camera," she moaned, "and this one flash gun."

"We can come back some other time," I suggested.

"You don't know how I worked to persuade her to do it," she reminded me. "And ten dollars is ten dollars."

"*Cassé?*" asked the *mambo,* and I could swear I saw a look of triumph in her elusive eyes.

"*Cassé!*" said Lorena tersely, turning the flash gun over and over in her hand. "*Cassé!*" Broken! But it really was not broken, it just didn't work.

The *mambo* pointed to the *veve.* "Agué," she said proudly.

"Yes, I see," I said. "*Belle, belle*—pretty." She laughed, pleased.

I was sure I would never forget Agué, guardian of the sea, keeper of the deep, whom Reser had once called the Voodoo Poseidon—Agué who rode the waves and watched the islands, who spotted every traveler that crossed the water and who very likely had had his eyes on us ever since we defied his domain by coming to Haiti by air.

"Agué Woyo," said the *mambo* giving the deity his full name and honoring him with a little song.

"Once more," Lorena ordered as she clamped fresh batteries into the flash gun and pressed the connection into place.

"*Enco?*" asked the *mambo.*

"*Enco,*" said Lorena. "It just *has* to work."

The *mambo* obligingly took another handful of meal with a remark that brought a smile to her assistant. Then she began to add an anchor to Agué's ship.

This time Lorena planted herself for a straightaway shot and said nothing when I unconcernedly propped my elbow on my hip and comfortably held the reflector in that position. Frankly I had not a bit of faith that the lights would work. They didn't. They failed on this fifth time and they were to fail on the fifteenth.

The *mambo* beamed her broadest, most wholesome smile when she said, "No? *Cassé?*"

"*Cassé,*" I said.

"This is the darndest thing I've ever had happen," Lorena concluded. "I had the Eastman people go over all of this before I came to Haiti, and they charged me twenty-five dollars. Said everything was perfect. This has certainly got me."

"*Veve bon, bon,*" said the *mambo* as she turned to admire her handiwork.

It was really quite ironical, Lorena with five hundred dollars' worth of equipment in her hands and yet unable to cope with Agué's corn-meal ship.

About this time a stranger appeared at an opening to our right. He was one of those small, wiry men, deeply black and of indeterminable age, dressed in light cotton pants and an open shirt. When the *mambo* saw him she explained to him what had been taking place, and her eyes were dancing as she related the story that something was *cassé.*

He chuckled and spoke to her in rapid Creole. She made a show of sadness and turned to us. From her hurried comments I caught the words *oto* and *kaotchou.*

Lorena looked at me. "Now what?"

"*Oto* is auto," I said, "and *kaotchou* is tire." I addressed the man. "*Pan?*" I asked.

"*Pan,*" he answered with a nod.

"*Pan,*" I repeated to Lorena, "means flat. Let's go."

In the glow of the flashlight I changed the *kaotchou* while a group of chattering children and a few adults watched amused, extemporizing about the trouble and toil of these *otos* yet marveling at every operation. Hopelessly Lorena stood there studying the expressive characters and the portrait possibilities, then looking disgustedly at her flash equipment. The mood of everyone was so festive and good-natured that I am sure the answer to her *Quitte um tiré portré ou, no?* would have been an enthusiastic Okay.

It was no use. We drove disconsolately to Port-au-Prince with Lorena assailing everyone from Agué down to the Eastman Company.

The following morning she took the Medalist and flash attachments to the camera shop of Mr. Kahn.

M'sieur Kahn, expert in the ways of handling both temperamental cameras and their owners, listened studiously to the complaint. "Well, let us see," he sighed. "Let us take a look at this thing."

He plugged the flash connection into the camera. Lorena held the extension. He tripped the shutter. There was a bright flash of light.

"Well, I'll be . . . !" Lorena exclaimed.

"It seems to work," drawled *M'sieur* Kahn. "It surely seems to work very well. We will try it again." He did. It worked perfectly. Five times. I was sure it would have worked as well for fifty or forever, for that matter.

"I see nothing wrong," concluded *M'sieur* Kahn. "Nothing at all."

"I'm going back to that place!" vowed Lorena. "And if I don't get a picture of that *mambo,* I'll know the reason why!"

"It was Agué who was the reason," I had to say. "Agué Woyo, god of the sea."

3.

Since we had trouble renting an *oto* during the next few days, we stayed in the capital city where I interviewed a number of people and ran into an amazing variety of ideas concerning Voodoo.

There was, for example, the businessman who had a museum of Voodoo artifacts in his mansion home. His possessions in this line ran all the way from curse charms, called *wangas* and *caprelateas,* to the most beautiful altar pieces I had ever seen. He had a complete record of the services he had attended when he came to Haiti years ago from Europe, pen-and-ink drawings of *veves* and rare accounts of Voodoo legends. To him Voodoo was partly a peasant's faith and partly witchcraft.

There was the executive who talked about Voodoo in hushed tones and said he once heard drums beating incessantly for three days and nights in the hills behind his Kenscoff home. Finally he called the police. They never found the drummers, but the drumming stopped. His feeling was one of concern.

There was the Englishman who said he was all in favor of Voodoo, for it was the natural religion and emotional expression of the people. He told me about a *houngan* named Duco who insisted that once he had been drowned in the Caribbean and that he lay for days at the bottom of the sea. Duco said that as he lay there he saw the shadow of a canoe. Then a man got out and walked on the water, reached down and rescued him. Nothing could dissuade Duco from believing that the Englishman had been his savior.

There was the doctor who related that he had been called to a shack in the hills by a peasant mother who said, "My child is dying." He found the eight-year-old girl mentally resigned to die, but his diagnosis revealed nothing organically wrong with the child, nor could he find any symptom of sickness. "She is going to die," said the mother. "A neighbor has asked a *mambo* to put a *wanga* on her." "Which neighbor?" asked the doctor. The mother pointed to the house. "Who put the *wanga* on her?" he asked. The mother gave him the name of an unscrupulous *mambo*.

The doctor called on the *mambo* and arranged that she put a counteracting *wanga* upon the child. "I will do so tomorrow morning at eight o'clock," the *mambo* told him. "The child will get better. I am sorry the neighbor got me to put the *wanga* on the child in the first place." At eight o'clock the doctor made it a point to go to the offending neighbor's house to see what would happen. The neighbor said she had not been able to sleep all night and promptly at eight o'clock broke down and said she could no longer stand the pressure of what she had done to the child. "The curse has been lifted," she cried. When the doctor went to the sick girl's home he found her up and well.

He told about a girl who at the age of fifteen went insane. He tried to help her, as did other doctors, without success. Finally he consulted a reputable *houngan* who told him to buy certain meals and libations and place them in given positions in the girl's room. This he did, and when the spirit possessed the girl in a violent mood she moved the things around and then lost consciousness under possession. When she awoke she was cured of her insanity. He said this happened eight years ago and that the girl had been perfectly rational ever since. The doctor took a middle course in Voodoo. "It has concepts which are intellectually challenging," he said, "but the faith has been corrupted generally, and there is a great deal of commercialization creeping in."

There was the professional dancer who owed much of his success to a Voodoo priest. It was a *houngan* who saw in him artistic expression and gave him ideas from Voodoo ceremonies for his choreography. The dancer reviewed his career, from dancing in the peristyle to a performance in Carnegie Hall, from Haitian jungles to Decca records! Jean Léon Destiné, known and loved by all Haiti, was developing a primitive faith into a classical art.

Yet none of these men were able to get me into Voodoo services. Many made the effort. I was with the Englishman on several evenings when we visited peristyles and *hounforts* only to be told that there was nothing going on. Always the doors were closed. Always there was suspicion, and we were ushered politely but firmly away.

Not even the German-American explorer, a linguist and a scholar, had any luck. His passion for Haiti bordered on Voodoomania. Back for his third visit within six years, he bargained and pleaded with *ligne* drivers to take us to a *hounfort* near Croix des Bouquets. When we arrived at the spot I had a feeling that a service had been planned but hastily called off. A few men sitting in the deserted *tonnelle* played dumb to our questions and shrugged vaguely at the German's attempt to convince them that he really believed in Voodoo.

I think he did believe in it. I spent almost an entire night listening to his justification of the faith and trying to keep up with the trip-hammer logic of his Teutonic mind.

"I've given religion and the idea of human sacrifice a lot

of thought," he persisted. "What are Christians complaining about? Didn't their God set the example? He's the one who had His own Son put to death. Can you help it if others want to do the same?"

He never really wanted an answer. I never had one to give him. His arguments, so far as he was concerned, were flawless. He said he was an agnostic, a humanist, a man who had given up the "claptrap of commercialized churches" long ago.

"The trouble with religion," he said prophetically, "is that nobody is willing to die for his faith any more. Everything has been made nice and easy. What do your priests do when they observe the sacrifice? They take a wafer, a nice sweet-tasting wafer, and a nice sweet glass of wine. My God, sacrifice is supposed to mean suffering! In the olden days when plagues fell upon people it was necessary to propitiate the gods. In those days men and women were ready to offer themselves as the holy victims. They were ready to be set apart and to be crucified. Now they aren't even ready to be set apart!"

I had the feeling that he believed a few good human sacrifices would remake the world! His theory was that the greater a man's devotion to the gods, the greater would be that man's sacrifice. But since he did not believe any God or gods could possibly be known or understood, I never quite knew where he stood in the theological scheme. Yet his point of view was clear. Every religion at one time or another had practiced human sacrifice: whether by throwing oneself from a great height to die on the rocks, as in India at the shrine of Kali; being set adrift alone in a boat, as among the American Indians; diving into a holy *cenote,* as among the Mayans; dying by the sword during an eclipse of the sun, as in parts of Mexico; or being crucified, it was all the same.

The interesting part about this Port-au-Prince poll on Voodoo was that I found no one who held the opinions set forth by Spenser St. John, Seabrook, Lindsay or any others who had written sensationally about it. Reser's statements came back to me. He had said, "Unfortunately, a sensational lie is more quickly believed than the sober truth. Rest assured that when a writer bases his remarks on one fanatical case of human sacrifice he is not talking about Voodoo as a people's faith. We are always tempted to scorn that which we do not understand."

There were, however, some men who claimed they understood Voodoo and who denounced it righteously. These were the representatives of the Protestant mission work: Methodist, Baptist, Pentecostal, Adventist. I was with some of these missionaries when they rode their circuits. I followed them up the steep, slippery paths of the mountains and through heavily wooded trails and I was convinced they believed in their calling. High up in isolated villages, they built their little churches out of the stuff of the hilltop. They equipped them with backless benches and homemade chairs with sisal seats. To beautify them they made bowers of palm fronds and poinsettias and festooned them with woven branches. Here they preached and taught, trying to bring a new ethical consciousness and a democratic faith to people who had never heard of the Protestant concept of a God of love. This the missionaries considered the great message. Their God was not to be feared or appeased but simply trusted and believed.

Voodoo to the missionaries was a curse. When a person became a Protestant he was expected to gather up his pagan paraphernalia—the drums, beads, pictures, robes, swords, *govis*, flags, charms and *assons*. A fire was lighted, a burning took place, and the last vestiges of the *loa* were committed to the flames.

"This is the difference between our attitude toward Voodoo and the Catholic attitude," a minister told me. "We demand that our converts cut clean and completely with this vicious cult. Catholicism simply tries to get its people to sign a *rejet,* a promise that they will have nothing more to do with Voodooism. The Catholic Church knows full well that even though the *rejet* is signed the people still keep their altars and jars. They worship Damballa during the week and Jesus on Sundays. We say, 'Come out from among them!' Catholicism says, 'We will educate them away from Voodoo.' How long do they expect this education to take? They have been trying for four hundred years, and Voodoo is still flourishing."

But even these Protestant zealots never claimed that Voodoo was cannibalism and human sacrifice. I could find no Haitians who spoke of it in those terms. Only outsiders related these fantastic accounts, only outsiders warned me as Paul Ramsey had done, only tourists had the "big stories about Voodoo." A man from Florida said he had never seen Voodoo in Haiti, but he certainly knew what it was like in Cuba. He related how a friend of his, disguised as a peon, got in on an annual Voodoo convocation in the mountains near the border of the province of Oriente.

"When the huge fire was built before an inconspicuous altar," he told me, "my friend hid in a clump of shrubbery. The *mamaloi* and *papaloi,* priest and priestess, appeared. The *mamaloi* did a *rumba,* and the people began to be aroused emotionally. Roosters and goats were sacrificed to the snake, and the snake was burned. Then the 'goat without horns' was brought out, a blonde white child apparently only a few months old. The priest took the sacrificial knife. He made two cuts into the breast, pulled out the heart, cut it open as if it were a coconut, drained the blood into a beautiful gem-encrusted chalice, and the sacrament was ready. This was the climax of the rite. After the sacrament came the drums and the dances. The crowd reached the end of endurance; then each leaped upon the most convenient of the opposite sex and satisfied the demand of the moment, until nude bodies scattered in the postures of their last excesses created a vision of hell worthy of Dante."

Had Haiti's sex-mad Voodoo moved to Cuba with the peasants who went over seeking easier work and better pay? Cannibal-Voodoo was always hearsay. Sex-Voodoo was always in the form of dramatized accounts. Orgiastic-Voodoo, as far as we could find, existed only in tall tales or had got confused with some of the country dances of Haiti, which have about as much connection with Voodoo as an American barn dance has with an evangelistic revival.

When we were able to rent an *oto* we looked for Voodoo services in the Plaine du Cul de Sac. Our search took us far beyond the asylum at Pont Beudet to the lonely village of Thomazeau where dismal homes set up around the dusty market street stood like temporary dwellings of a nomadic tribe. It led us to the sacred falls of Saut d'Eau where throughout the year the faithful come to climb the rocky stairs of the cascade. If there is a waterfall in Paradise, it must be another Saut d'Eau. To feel the magic spray is Voodoo's christening, to bathe in the falls is as lucky as touching the waters of the Ganges or the Nile.

We looked for the mad, bad Voodoo in Mirebalais, Lorena's happiest hunting ground. She shot everything in sight from ancient cemetery to incongruous Coca-Cola sign, from *tonnelle* to the new and modest Protestant church.

There are people in Mirebalais who will not quickly forget us, for it was in this carless village that my *oto* horn got stuck and summoned half the populace with its twenty minutes of steady barking. They will remember the white man who could not even find the source of the honking hidden under the radiator grilling and did not know that the Creole word for horn is simply *klaxon*. The only mechanic in the village will remember how he silenced the *klaxon* permanently with a monkey wrench.

We looked continually for Voodoo's frantic excesses and failed to find them. We failed even to find any evidence of them. Whenever we were shown an altar with curse charms—*wangas*—we were also shown good-luck charms or *paquets*. The first were shapeless black "dolls" sewn with feathers and sometimes with human hair. They were stuffed with many things: ashes, graveyard dirt, magic leaves, sulphur and salt. The power of the *wangas* was said to be relentless and avenging—the protection of the *paquets* certain and sure. All of which seemed to me nothing more than an attempted explanation of the eternal warfare between good luck and bad, a warfare that uses individuals indiscriminately as its battleground.

4.

THEN one day I received a call from a friend, a Port-au-Prince businessman. He telephoned to say that a peasant had brought a load of merchandise on his back from the Artibonite country near Saint Marc. The peasant, whose name was Ti Toma, had told him he was returning immediately because of a Voodoo service in his village on the following evening.

"I can get him to stay overnight" was the announcement. "If you want to take him back tomorrow, he can perhaps get you into the service. I have no idea whether this will be worth while or not."

"Are you going along?" I asked.

"Not on your life," he said. "But you can use my jeep, if you wish."

"I may take you up on that," I said. "*Otos* are hard to get."

"There's just one thing," he added. "Ti Toma knows no English."

"Not even as much as I do Creole?"

"Not even that little!" was the answer.

"We'll still go," I said, and Lorena agreed.

Ti Toma was not a man we would have chosen without a reference. He was in his late thirties, small but strongly built. The flesh of his arms seemed all muscle and his face was jet-black. His nose was flat and his eyes were wide-spaced against high cheek bones. On his left temple was a small scar, like an old knife cut, running under his crinkly hair. Most disconcerting was a kind of suspicion he seemed to have about us and a stubborn attitude that spoke of resentment, as if he had been talked into something against his will and was just now catching on. He made believe that he could not understand our Creole at all. Lorena figured we probably did not have the Artibonite accent!

What worried me was that he might actually be able to understand our English, for sometimes when Lorena and I carried on a conversation he brooded as if stoically absorbing all that was said. It bothered me that he never smiled. Our friend, the merchant, had assured us, however, that Ti Toma was reliable and that he had consented to take us to the service. What kind of a service? All we could get out of him on that score was *kabrit*. That meant goat.

We drove to Saint Marc and, after our experiences with roads to other locations in this land where four fifths of the area is mountains, found this drive between the two seaport cities easy—easy and consistently picturesque. Yet no matter where one goes in Haiti, a kilometer is always longer than a mile. It should not be, but its 3,280.8 feet keep growing and unfolding, especially when next to one is the shadow of an impassive black face watching yet not watching, listening yet not listening, giving no indication of what is going on in his mind.

We stopped for kola and something to eat. It apparently was immaterial to our companion whether he ate or not, whether we talked to him or were silent, or even whether we continued on our journey or turned around and went home. Whenever Lorena stopped to take pictures he glanced at us dubiously but gave no other indication of what he was thinking. Cigarettes were our most satisfactory means of communication, and fortunately I had an extra large supply. I continued urging them upon him until the sun began to lose itself within the chains of mountains.

It was at about this time that Ti Toma became vocal and showed signs of interest. He guided us to a road that turned off the graveled highway. It was rocks and plain and scrub which had not seen an *oto* since the rains washed it out. It was, in turn, mountainside, dried-out river basin and a faint track leading into nothing but trouble. It was a trail built strictly for people like Ti Toma who traveled on foot. Nothing but a jeep could have maneuvered the darkening and uncertain passages, and sometimes I wondered if ours could possibly go on. We could have walked as fast as we were riding. Incessantly we asked our companion in our best Creole, *"Li loin toujou?"* (Is it much more?)

He had a typical peasant's answer. *"Pa pré, pa lwe."* (It isn't near and it isn't far.)

He was, of course, absolutely right. According to the speedometer, a kilometer was still the prescribed number of feet; according to our agony, a thousand miles. But at any rate, Ti Toma was beginning to talk and his voice had a touch of veiled eagerness, a kind of thrill as if he were nearing home and, for the first time, in an *oto.*

One thing was in our favor—the night was fully tropical. A steel-white moon was already casting a sheen of brilliant glory across the heavens. There was always something about a night like this that filled me with confidence, confidence in the people and in the land. But this once I longed desperately for Reser, hoping that by some Voodoo magic he would suddenly appear.

Lorena's frequent "What do you think?" showed her concern. She was reading my thoughts. I was asking myself whether we should try to go on or attempt something equally difficult—turn around. I said, "Reser claims a man can cross Haiti day or night and find friends. He is never alone. A hundred feet into the jungle, a short walk into the hills, there is always someone there."

Just now this was questionable comfort. I reflected on my merchant friend whose jeep had been entrusted to me. Would he have suggested a mission such as this if it had not been perfectly safe? I was not so sure. He was very likely saying, "If they are crazy enough to go after this Voodoo business, let them get their fill of it."

Hanging on to the wheel, wondering how much longer the *oto* would hold out I asked aloud, "How much more?"

"It isn't near and it isn't far," said Lorena, trying to make a joke out of it. I liked her spirit and her unfailing sense of humor and told her to give Ti Toma another cigarette. She gave him another package.

Then we came to a village with houses that looked like silver umbrellas in the moonlight. There was the sight of a small fire burning in a swept-out yard, and there were a few figures moving. Here, the jungle had been pushed aside by man's hand. Here, a whiteness was moving—the whiteness of dresses and headbands.

"Icite, icite!" exclaimed Ti Toma and he meant, Here, stop here! He meant, Shut off the motor and let's get out. We are home!

"What shall I do about the cameras?" asked Lorena.

"You can't leave them," I said. "You can't take them."

"That's the way I feel," she agreed.

"I'll take one," I suggested. "You take the other. Leave the flash equipment here. If it's gone, it's gone. No pictures tonight. I don't know what we're getting into."

"Bonsoir," we greeted as we got out and stretched our legs.

"Bonsoir," said a number of the people.

Ti Toma turned from a small group to whom he had been talking and motioned to us. *"Vini!"* Come! We went to him.

"Oto?" I asked. "Okay?"

"Okay," said Ti Toma.

I gave the jeep a glance and committed it to the *loa*.

Then I heard the drums. Their subterranean throbbing quaked and flowed through the patchwork of shacks. Somehow it was a good sound, a rewarding sound. The *ogan* argued with its high-pitched beep-beep. The chanting of the worshipers drove my lurking fears away. Ti Toma was noticeably more solicitous. He grinned at us for the first time as if to say we had made it—late but still in time. The thought occurred to me that he may have been as wary of us along the trip as we had been of him. We often had our feelings of distrust about the natives, but how about their distrust of us? After all, we were the intruders, not they; we the invaders, the spies. What were our motives? Why should they put their confidence in an *Americain?*

"Ti Toma," I said, *"youn moma."* (One moment!)

I hurried back to the jeep and got a carton of cigarettes. These I gave to him, making him understand they were for the drummers. He was pleased. *"Merci, merci! E l'houngan?"*

I tried to make clear that we would show our appreciation to the *houngan* in another way, and apparently he understood.

Eagerly we followed him to the *tonnelle*. Its roof sparkled like tinsel. Its portals were mysterious passageways within which we saw the flicker of lights and rows of people. Ti Toma gabbled happily to himself and led us in.

We entered so unobtrusively that we would never have been noticed had we been black. No one would have paid any attention to us—but we were white. The awareness of our presence was mentally telegraphed among the worshipers. A hundred pairs of eyes took cognizance of the fact that we were

white, that we were in the canopied shelter, that we were with
Ti Toma. The *houngan,* a wizened man in a ceremonial man-
tle, saw us. His *asson* paused a moment, but the drummers
never missed a beat.

It was a Voodoo setting: the drummers and the *ogantier,* the
festooned center pole and the cluttered altar, the smell of cologne and rum, the scent of the earth, the rattle of the *asson* and
the ringing of the bell, the chanting *hounsi* adorned in their
sacred necklaces, and the swaying bodies.

This time we saw a new inclusion—*l'kabrit*. The black goat
with a red robe draped over its back was nibbling at a scattered
pile of fresh green leaves.

I longed for Reser. I would have given a good deal for his
strong presence and the benefit of his knowledge. He would
have read meaning into the liturgy which now ran its lengthy
cycles. He would have explained the *veve* which the *houngan*
drew with well-timed strokes upon the ground. The libations
and the ceremonies at the altar needed a priest's interpretation,
and I would have been grateful for Reser's views on *l'kabrit*.

The goat's role, however, was quite apparent. *La place* was
lifting off the robe. *L'kabrit* looked up startled as if for the first
time it had a premonition of what was to come. The *hounsi*
came forward with bowls and jars. The scent of cologne rose
in a sweet savor as they sprinkled perfume on *l'kabrit*. The
odor sharpened the senses of the worshipers. The staccato mé-
lange of the drums evoked a cross fire of emotional cries. As
if summoned by these intoxicating sounds, a woman became
possessed. The *loa* mounted her, and she whirled furiously. In
a moment she flung herself upon the goat and clung to it with
her arms about its neck. She tried to ride it, but *la place* held

the animal, and the *houngan* came to the woman and controlled her with his words, so that she soon released the goat and went dancing and shouting out into the night.

Once more *l'kabrit* was perfumed. Then a sash was fastened around its neck and *la place* preceded by the *houngan* led it round and round the center pole. This developed into a triumphal march with *hounsi,* flag-bearers and worshipers chanting and half dancing to the spell of the drums. In such a ritual man, since the beginning of time, had laid his sins upon some traditional totemic animal and driven it into the wilderness, driven it with all of his guilt and offense to show the gods that this was his vicarious sacrifice. In this way the great god Pan and the satyrs took the form of goats. In such a gathering the ideas of redemption and forgiveness had their origins among believing people ages ago. Or perhaps instead of causing *l'kabrit* to wander with the sins of humanity laid upon him, the ancients, too, watched and waited, as we did now while the saber-bearer presented the sharp sword to the dancing priest.

As I saw all of this I felt what Reser must so often have experienced, the thrill of linking past belief to present seeking, the lure of reading into these ancient acts the graphic meaning of concepts that have persisted in cultures everywhere. A whir of texts flashed into mind, phrases about shed blood and lambs led to the slaughter. Now the *houngan* held a bottle in his hand as if it were a chalice. He took a long drink. Ti Toma looked at me and nodded as if hoping that I saw the deep significance in all of this. I felt a sudden nearness to him.

Lorena sat upright, oblivious of us. Something more authoritative than a human voice was evidently telling her that pictures were out. The emotion of the people was like a vapor rising. They had forgotten about us as they had become absorbed in the scene before them. Then in an instant, with a speed that almost escaped my attention, the sword flashed. There was a cry from the chanting group, and *l'kabrit's* quivering body fell. But not before black hands had deftly seized it and held it during its death spasm. A woman with a bowl caught the gushing blood.

Would she drink it? Did the *houngan* put his lips to the bowl? I could not say. Confusion broke over the scene and hid from me whatever bloody ritual was in progress. Just now it was difficult for me not to think that my own religious culture was far superior to that which I was witnessing. I was the observer looking down from the watchtower of my faith. For a moment pity and abhorrence stole my thoughts. Then the drum, the voices, the clapping hands and the dancing figures made me wonder anew whether these worshipers questioned or had the least doubt about the rightness of their own practices. Was my concept better because it was different or because it was newer? The words of the German, who said that the Christian's God had demanded not a goat but His own Son, were oddly confusing. The link was worship. To each, his own way. The link was faith. To every man, the interpretation which to him was honest and right. Belief makes it right to the believer.

Ti Toma was a good surety. Sensing that we depended upon him he gave us by word and expression the confidence we needed. He lighted a cigarette and indicated that he would remain an observer rather than a participant for our sakes. But he did something more. He suggested by his intense interest that we should try to understand that the climax of the service was not the killing of the goat, but, rather, the transference of an impression upon the worshipers. What kind of an impression? That God and man had been reconciled by the blood. That the goat belonged to the *loa* as much as to mortals. It must naturally follow that *l'kabrit* played the part of a human sacrifice, and extreme reverence must be attached to the act.

The service proceeded, having, it seemed to me, much the same relationship to this sacrifice that the Postcommunion has to the Mass. There were prayers of thanksgiving and chants of praise. Catholicism was once more grafted upon Voodoo, and Christian saints were again interwoven with the great names of the *mystère*.

The carcass of *l'kabrit* wrapped in its red robe was taken from the *tonnelle;* the altar properties were returned to their rightful places; already the illusion was being created that what had taken place had been magical and unreal. Slowly cleanliness and order were achieved in the place of worship. Gradually the surroundings became hushed. The *veve* had disappeared. It was all like a dream, like something working behind the phenomenon, like going upon the stage after the master of illusion has completed his act, like stepping into the sanctuary after the mystery of transubstantiation has been performed and seeing only the altar and the things that hands have made.

We went up to give the drummers the cigarettes and to show our appreciation to the silently evasive *houngan*. As for Ti Toma, when we tried to pay him, he would take nothing. It was difficult for us to understand this new attitude. Why did he help us get the car close to his palm-thatched home and make it possible for us to sleep on mats near by? Why did he show us the following morning how the roasted meat of the sacrifice was distributed to the people and how some of it was placed at the crossroads for Kalfu? And why did he insist on accompanying us back to the highway at Saint Marc? There could be only one reason. Ti Toma must have felt the same secret affection for us that we had learned to have for him. Our farewells were fervent. He stood watching us as we headed the jeep toward Port-au-Prince. He waved to us as though we had been his long-time friends, and that is how we felt as we drove away.

This, too, was Voodoo.

5.

EXCEPT for our excursion with Ti Toma, we had no luck. Two weeks of independent research convinced me that I could get nowhere without Reser. Some whites in Haiti had large collections of Voodoo artifacts and altar pieces. Some had made it a point to learn the songs and chants. Others looked at it as a psychological study, had kept records of services, knew several priests and priestesses and could even recite the names of the *loa* in the Voodoo pantheon. But Reser was the only one who lived behind the scenes. Others observed it; he was in it.

I did not always tell people that I had been with him on Voodoo trips, but frequently his name came up. I was told that he had been seen more than once possessed. During a service at Croix des Bouquets he picked up the *asson* and sang a hymn to one of the *loa*. The *loa* mounted him, and he started down the

road. Many people followed, for he was marvelously transformed. It was not he who was walking. It was Guedé. Everyone knew it was Guedé, because his head was wrapped in a
black bandanna and he moved with a jumping motion. He
gossiped incessantly, talking through his nose. He looked like
Guedé, and those who saw him felt that they were close to
Death, but Guedé made fun of them and joked with them to
make them laugh. But they did not laugh, for one does not
laugh at Guedé.

Fred Alsop, assistant manager of the airport, and a friend
spied Reser on this occasion and went to speak to him, but it
was Guedé they were talking to, and Guedé could speak only
Creole. At four o'clock in the morning when Guedé finally left
his mount, Reser found himself walking in the cemetery in
Port-au-Prince. How he got there he did not know. Later the
friend met him and said, "I sure wish I could get hold of some
of that stuff that you were tanked up with that night. You were
in great shape!" But those who knew the *loa* knew that it was
Guedé and called it a mighty visitation.

All of this convinced me that it was time I saw him again, and
I decided to bury my pride and go back to the Chez Pauline.

The trip was unnecessary. I was waiting for a *ligne* in
downtown Port-au-Prince when a sudden rain hit the city, a
November rain, warm and caressing. I ducked into Higgins'
Bar to wait it out and was immediately greeted by a shout of
welcome above the crazy booming of drums. In the center of
the room sat Reser and Ti Roro, one of Haiti's foremost drummers. Reser was whooping things up on a large *maman* drum
and the younger man played the smaller *cata*. At the tables
Haitians and tourists leaned over their glasses listening as if

they never intended to leave. I felt the same way. I was seeing another Stanley Reser, an entertainer of high talent, who was being applauded fully as much as was the happily grinning Ti Roro.

The customers at the bar called out their requests. The bartender leaned contentedly against the liquor shelf while his assistant wiped the bar in keeping with the rhythm. People who had come in to escape the rain stood about: poorly clad men and well-dressed men in white Palm Beach—a cross section of the Port-au-Prince populace, a slice of life typical of the capital city.

Reser, better than anyone, knew that these people, particularly the peasants, lived constantly on the edge of joy. So did he, for that matter. It needed only a drum and a knowledge of songs to push a crowd into the wonder-world of forgetfulness. This show had been going on for some time. *Clairin* bottles and empty rum glasses indicated that they had helped put the glow on this matinee, but the star billing was *M'sieur* Doc. I could not possibly have met him under more favorable circumstances. He was rhythm incarnate. His body was swaying with the syncopated music of the painted drums. He sang American folk songs to African drumbeats and African chants to American jazz. He sang songs of the sea which belonged to every race, and gospel hymns which could be claimed by every faith.

A thin-haired, deeply tanned fellow next to me, who looked as though he had just stepped off a yacht in the harbor, said, "Who in God's name is this man?"

I was asking myself the same question, for Reser's glances at me were warm invitations to come back into the fold. Any

discord of the past was forgotten, and all was forgiven. He
even dedicated a song to me:

> *"Li entré avec le division,*
> *Bonsoiré!*
> *Li entré avec le division,*
> *Bonsoiré!*
> *Trois coups d'canons,*
> *Trois coups nacional,*
> *Quitte l'entré,*
> *Bonsoiré!"*

> He comes in with the company,
>   Good evening!
> He comes in with the company,
>   Good evening!
> Three salvos from the cannon,
> Three salvos from the squadron,
> Let him come in!
>   Good evening!

The thin rattle of rain upon the windows was like finger taps
of the *loa* trying to get in. The steady splashing on the pave-
ment sent a fine spray through the open door like mist from
the Saut d'Eau. This was Haiti: carefree, fatalistic, christened
of the gods; knowing no poverty, greed or pain; having no time
for such petty things as local or international treachery; estimat-
ing for the moment no differences between black and white;
bewitched by the magnetism of the drums, and enchanted by a
love for life.

Reser rose to his feet. He snapped his fingers and said, *"Cric!"*
Several Haitians responded, *"Crac!"* A hush fell over the room.
It was the signal for a story, a challenge for a raconteur to match

his talent with the allurement of rain and rum and prove to the world that there are no folk tales like the fables of the Magic Isle.

In faultless Creole the white man said, "I will tell you the story entitled 'Ti Malice Goes to Confession.'"

One Easter Sunday, not so many years ago, Ti Malice decided to do his Easter duties. Before leaving home he made sure that he had his money with him, for the church members had recently voted that everyone going to confession should give fifty centimes toward building a new chapel. Ti Malice went to church and when his turn came knelt before the lattice in the booth.

"Father," said Malice, "I don't know whether I have sinned or not, but I did something the other day I want to ask you about. As I was going down a lane I saw a rope alongside the fence. When I picked it up and tried to walk off with it I found that it was tied to a goat on the other side of the fence. I pulled, but the hole in the fence was not big enough for the goat to come through. So I dropped the rope and went home. Now I want to know if that's a sin."

"You tried to take the goat, did you not?"

"Yes, father."

"If the hole in the fence had been big enough you would have stolen the goat, would you not?"

"Yes, father!"

"Well, then, Malice, my son, you have sinned. You tried to steal the goat and failed through no fault of your own. It was just the same as if you had stolen that goat."

Malice told the Lord he was sorry, and the priest gave him absolution. Then he took the fifty-centime piece from his pocket and offered it to the priest through one of the holes in the lattice. The priest took hold of the money and tried to pull it through, but the square was just a little too small.

"Come around to the side and give it to me," said the priest.

"Pardon me, father," Malice spoke up, "you tried to take the money, didn't you?"

"Why, yes, what of it?" replied the priest in astonishment.

"If the hole had been big enough, you would have taken it, wouldn't you?"

"Yes, yes, what are you trying to get at?"

"Only this, father. You just told me that when I tried to pull the goat through the fence it was just the same as if I had stolen it. Now you tried to pull the money through the square, and it is just the same as if you had it in your pocket. Good morning, father!"

Malice turned and left the church. The priest was speechless with astonishment.

"And so, my good friends, ends the story of 'Ti Malice Goes to Confession.' "

Cric!

Crac!

6.

BACK with Reser we were again in the heart of things. Lorena and I spent an evening with him going over our experiences in an effort to put them into a reasonable perspective against the backdrop of Voodoo in Haiti. He fitted all the pieces together nicely without resenting the fact that we had gone out on an independent search without him. He greeted Lorena's story of the flash-that-wouldn't-go-off with an amused, "Oh-o!" The fact that we had probed into the Voodoo theories of the elite of Port-au-Prince and had found no violent denunciation of the faith pleased him.

Our trip to Mirebalais, Saut d'Eau and Thomazeau was interpreted by him as a tourists' jaunt.

He registered more interest when we described the sacrifice of *l'kabrit*. I asked him whether he had ever seen the blood of a sacrifice consumed by the priest or *mambo*. He said he had not.

"What is done with the blood?" I asked.

"Sometimes mystical signs are made with it. Frequently it is used for food."

"Food?" asked Lorena.

"Haven't you ever eaten *Blutwurst?*" he wanted to know. "That's a good German product."

"Sure, I've eaten it," I said.

"Well, that's blood sausage. I see no difference if the blood of a sacrifice is occasionally used for food." Then he became thoughtful. "Don't ever go to north Haiti without me," he warned. "I can show you services that have never been seen by outsiders. There is, for example, *Mange Marassa,* a sacrifice to the spirit of the twins. In the cosmic system Voodoo has its Papa and Mama Marassa, who are the parents of the twins of the universe. People in south Haiti serve the *loa,* in the north they serve Marassa. Marassa is the foundation of the universe. Before he kills you, Death asks permission of the Marassa. Don't go to north Haiti without me!"

"We don't intend to go anywhere without you," said Lorena.

"Bon, bon!" he answered, pleased.

I think it was that expression and the way he said it that put the seal upon our new friendship and started us on a series of Voodoo adventures. It was on this very night that I had an appointment with the Jamaican *"mambo."*

"Do you know this woman?" I asked, mentioning her name.

"Slightly. Very slightly."

"Lorena just told you we won't go anywhere without you. Will you come along to this service?"

"If the Jamaican woman doesn't object," he said agreeably.

"I'll tell her we want you there."

"Oh-o!" he said.

I understood the meaning of his enigmatical byword when I visited the woman in her sisal shop.

"You are coming tonight, aren't you?" she greeted. "And your wife?"

"We are planning to. I'd like permission to bring one other person."

"An American?" she asked.

"In a way. Stanley Reser."

Her face changed expression. "Doc Reser?" she asked.

"Doc Reser."

"You know him?"

"Quite well."

"He—is your friend?"

"Quite a good friend," I said.

"Why do you want to bring him?"

"He seems to know a great deal about Voodoo."

"So do I," she retorted.

"I didn't mean to insinuate that you didn't!"

"Have you told him about this service?"

"Yes."

At once she became very cordial. "Well, if you have told him," she said, "bring him by all means."

"Do *you* know him?"

"I think most people know Doctor Reser. Yes, bring him along. Please do."

The house at which the meeting was scheduled was a modest frame dwelling at the outskirts of the city at Post Marchand. At nine o'clock when Lorena, Reser and I approached the open door we saw through the hallway a tall, slender, gray-haired woman bending over a corner altar. Near by sat a studious-appearing young man, two girls of perhaps eighteen and twenty, two middle-aged women and two men. Our Jamaican friend was hovering over the altar apparently directing the placement of the sacred articles.

I rapped on the doorpost. The young man greeted us in English. Then he carried on a brief conversation with Reser in French, and I assumed that they had met before.

He ushered us into the rather cramped room and introduced us to the group. Reser was soon conversing amiably in French with everyone leading me to believe that he was well known to the household. The gray-haired woman was the hostess; the young man, her son-in-law; the girls, her daughters; and the others were neighbors who had come in for the service.

When Reser was presented to the Jamaican woman there was an exchange of greetings in Creole, but I saw no signs like those which usually passed between him and initiates of the Voodoo society. They spoke together for a short time and then the *"mambo"* said, "Since you are here, Doctor Reser, why don't you take charge?"

"By no means!" was the reply. "No doubt you have a definite purpose in mind for the service. I came along merely because I want my friends to understand what is happening."

This laconic statement caused the woman to study him for a moment and then turn away. She went to the altar and lighted seven wicks in a plate of oil. This was a signal for everyone to find places in the room. Chairs were provided, and Lorena and I sat with Reser between us.

Rattling the *asson,* the *"mambo"* began a song saluting Legba, in which all joined. There were no drums and no *ogan* at this service. Our little group reminded me of the old-time family altars once traditional in American homes. As I sat in this Voodoo meeting I thought of neighborhood gatherings which I had attended as a boy in the Bible Belt. By a simple change in hymnody, this could just as well have been a Protestant get-together. We needed only the substitution of "Come, Thou Almighty King" for "Come, Papa Legba," and a good, old-fashioned family prayer for the litany to the *loa* to take me back to a room in my uncle's home. The "Our Father" was interchangeable, only here it was in Creole instead of in Midwestern English. Like my old aunt who used to conduct these cottage revivals, the Jamaican leader displayed a righteous enthusiasm and indicated that unless we got stirred up emotionally the spirits would pass us by. The *action de grâce,* prayers and rituals leading to Voodoo were not too different from the familiar invocations in the home where the Holy Spirit was often called upon.

Memory carried the analogy even further. I remembered one time when the preacher dropped in on one of our neighborhood meetings. That was the only time my aunt was flustered. Here, in this Voodoo meeting, Reser's presence was akin to that of a visiting cleric. For the first time in my experience the confident Jamaican faltered in the ritual.

It was apparent even to Lorena and me that she was confused. What had apparently started as a Petro service was leading into a ceremony which belonged to an altogether different family of *loa*. It was like starting a service to Saint Peter and inadvertently switching it to Saint Paul! It was like a priest taking liberties with the Mass, and I soon heard a stern voice at my side.

"No, it's this way!" Reser corrected her and brought her back on the proper ritualistic path.

She looked at him half-helplessly, half-gratefully, made another attempt and finally asked him to take charge. He went back over the invocations, led the singing and built the service to a pitch that invited possession. Then he asked the *"mambo"* to take over again for reasons that were explained to me when he returned to his chair. It seemed that this service had been called because the lady of the house had run into a cycle of bad luck. Madame's affairs were in such a state that she needed divine aid. This the Jamaican woman had promised to secure, and it was now up to her to produce results.

Soon the *"mambo"* called upon the *loa*. The moments passed. Occasionally she faded into a state of semi-trance. Then she shook herself, attended to ritualistic duties at the altar, poured out libations and tossed rice and roasted corn to the four cardinal points. A minute later her dancing motion increased. Gradually her antics grew more violent. All at once she seized a chair, sat down on it backward and made believe she was rowing and rocking in the sea.

"Agué!" someone said.

This recognition caused the rocking to increase until the chair was jumping energetically around the room. Then Agué left her. Again she poured rum and kola to the cardinal points. This done, she looked as if she were in the throes of a severe inner struggle. Her face contorted. She whimpered like a child. One could see by the way she tossed her head and spoke that she was simulating the characteristics of a young girl. Her grimaces caused the gray-haired hostess to become highly agitated. In a moment the hostess, too, jumped up and spoke in the same voice as that used by the *"mambo."* They quarreled and laughed and wept together, and I heard someone in the room say, "The Marassa!" Evidently they were being possessed by the Twins, identical *loa,* who are supposed to be governed by a single soul.

The impersonations went on for some time with constant dialogue passing between the two. Reser sat with his hands on his knees observing every move and listening to every word. Suddenly he folded his arms. My eyes fell upon the tattooed dragon. The gray-haired hostess looked at him, too. I do not know whether anything more than a glance passed between them, but she became almost instantly rational. Then as she stood there her body became rigid, and she was seized with a violent trembling. Her personality began to change. An alarming transformation took place, which caused the *"mambo"* to throw off her characterization of a Twin. The hostess was becoming powerfully possessed. Breathlessly we watched the transmutation, the invasion of the outside force, the emergence of the normal personality with its features and its character side by side, for a moment, with the intruding force; then it yielded, leaving the second in its place. The fear arose among us that this would be some demoniacal spirit, but it assumed a degree of holiness and sensitivity. The *loa* had mounted her, and his will was becoming the will of the possessed.

At my side I heard the familiar "Oh-o!" and the added comment, "It is Ogoun Badagri!"

Ogoun Badagri—he who gives advice and knowledge—was riding his horse. He drank generous quantities of rum. He danced and prophesied and made believe that he was the mightiest of the *loa.* He gave orders and instructions to his mount and called upon us to honor him with a song.

Salué Nago-é,
Nago rive-é,
Salué Nago-é,
Nago rive-é.
Li ler li tard o-o-o.
Li ler li tard é é é.
Salué Nago-é,
Jodila-o-o.

Salute Nago,
Nago has arrived,
Salute Nago,
Nago has arrived.
It is the hour.
It is late.
Salute Nago,
Today.

As we sang and clapped our hands, feeling that divine inter-
cession had come into the woman's life, her older daughter began to quiver and roll her eyes. Reser looked at the *"mambo"* as
if to call her attention to this phenomenon. Apparently she did
not see this or else did not know how to proceed. The girl was
obviously trying to give herself over to possession, but something
restrained her.

Reser got up. He strode across the room, passed the possessed
woman and put his hands on the girl's head. Immediately she
became possessed, and bedlam broke loose in the little room.
Flinging herself against the *"mambo,"* against chairs and
against the wall the girl spoke in a pyrotechnic of Creole and
assailed her mother who was now actually Ogoun Badagri.

Reser, meanwhile, returned to his chair. He showed me a
hairpin in his hand which he had taken out of the girl's hair.

"It was this," he explained, "that was holding back the *loa*. Metal will do that."

I looked up in time to see Ogoun Badagri strike the girl a sharp blow across the face. It evoked from her a taunting laugh. Then Ogoun grabbed the girl by the hair and swung her around. Next he threw a bowl of water on her. Insensible to these abuses, she struggled against her mother hysterically. Apparently there was meaning in all this which I did not see. Reser explained that some deep-seated altercation between mother and daughter was being resolved. The issues which they had refused to face realistically in their normal relationships were now being brought into the open by the *loa*. Their subconscious selves were meeting for the first time. Voodoo was revealing what had been hidden in the masquerade of life.

The argument was so loud and so prolonged that I expected the *gendarmerie* to appear at the open door any moment. Why the neighborhood did not come rushing over was a question that could be answered only by saying that Voodoo is Voodoo and everyone understood it.

We watched and listened to the battle of the *loa* from our ringside seats for at least thirty minutes, following as best we could the drama of possession and the perverse and reckless tactics which the *loa* employed to gain their ends. I could hear Lorena plying Reser with questions which he answered calmly, explaining that it was good to observe these things in all their many manifestations.

Patiently we watched, and finally Ogoun Badagri clasped the girl affectionately in a warm embrace. Then the *loa* departed. The invading personalities retreated; the identities of the participants returned. Mother and daughter looked at each other and realizing they were in each other's arms were mildly surprised. They turned their eyes to us as if asking what had happened. The girl was embarrassed that her wet hair hung about her face, but the mother smiled as if feeling a sense of inner peace.

We sang a song, during which the *"mambo"* took from the altar a huge bowl of steamed rice mixed with beans, peppers and corn. This was passed around the circle and each of us took a handful and consumed it. Then kola was supplied with rum for those who wanted it. We were expected to consume the dish of rice, handful after handful, leaving only enough to fill a calabash bowl, which would later be placed at a crossroad for Kalfu.

We ate and drank and visited, and after an hour of fellowship the *"mambo"* asked everyone to stand for a song and benedictory prayer. The "home revival" was over. Two of the worshipers had come "under conviction." When our Jamaican friend shook hands with us she assured us that these had been true possessions, but she looked at Reser as if there were many questions she wanted to ask.

Lorena asked the questions as we walked the long way back to town. *"M'sieur* Doc," she said, "there are a few things I want to know."

"Shoot!" he answered with a laugh. "I know just what they are."

"What?"

"Is this Voodoo?"

"Right," said Lorena. "Is it?"

"Well, I'll tell you," he replied, "I think the two possessions were genuine. I also think that the relationship between mother and daughter will be better now and the mother's affairs will work themselves out. She received some good advice from Ogoun Badagri."

"Do you think the Jamaican is really a *mambo?*" I asked.

"I think she is trying," he said seriously, "but she has a long way to go. She is like some so-called psychics who rely on intuition and their own power. When something happens that is really the work of spirit force, as it did tonight, they are bewildered. I'll tell you how this woman impresses me. She is like a person walking in the dark getting occasional flashes of lightning to guide her. Someday the lightning will really strike her, and then she will know what it is all about."

"Which brings me to the question," I said, "when are *we* going to know what it is all about? How long before you are going to take us behind the scenes?"

His answer was immediate. "From here on," he said, "I am going to show you all I dare show anyone. I think you are ready for it. Get an *oto,* and tomorrow we will go to meet the man whom I consider the most competent *houngan* in all of Haiti."

This was what we had been waiting to hear, and I held my breath when Lorena eagerly asked, "And pictures?"

Her persistence amused him. "Bring your cameras along," he said, "but this time take only what I tell you to take and *when* I tell you."

"That's a bargain!" Lorena agreed. "There'll be no snap of the shutter without your okay!" It was too dark for me to see her face, but her tone convinced even me that she meant it.

Chapter 5

THE PLANTATION OF THE VOODOO priest was located on the Plaine de Léogane some sixty kilometers southwest of Port-au-Prince. The house hemmed in by wooded foothills at a turn of the road was so inconspicuous I would never have taken it to be the abode of an *houngan extraordinaire*. It reminded me of the vine-covered cottage in which Reser lived. Towering coconut palms bent reverently over the corrugated-tin roof. Mango trees added shade and beauty to the yard.

Across the narrow road was a winding path that led to a long, thatch-roofed peristyle near which was an enormous mapou tree whose majestic buttresses reached out like muscular arms and whose large surface roots were giant snakes writhing away in all directions. The tree sacred to Damballa was wider at its trunk than the horse standing broadside against it. A cane mill stood prominently in a clearing, and many small but well-built huts were tucked away in the thick green growths.

A few children playing in the yard came up to the car when we pulled to the side of the road. Reser immediately delighted them with his Creole quips, and they clustered around us as we walked toward the house. A middle-aged woman came out of the screened-in porch to greet us and graciously poured out

Creole welcomes that even Lorena and I could understand. It was midafternoon, and naturally we would be staying for supper. Naturally we would be staying for *days*. She let it be known that a visit from *Docteur* Reser was an event and made us feel that the plantation and all it held was ours for the asking.

Two other women called greetings to us. They were working in the *ajupa,* the wattle-walled summer kitchen. Soon they came out, one carrying a baby against her breast. Other children hurried in from the groves. A man with a driving stick waved a welcome as he guided an ox team drawing a load of sugar cane out of the field.

Reser pointed out various sights to us, explaining to us and to the children, half in Creole and half in English, significant points about the vegetation bursting with tropical splendor. Directly behind the house was a magnificent calabash tree on which were hanging large gourds like green rubber balloons.

"In the time of Christophe," Reser explained, "all gourds were declared the property of the state and became the medium of exchange. The *gourde,* unit of modern Haitian currency, gets its name from that edict. What would we do without the wonderful calabash tree? When the gourd is large enough for use it is picked off, and a small hole is cut in the top, through which most of the contents are removed with a long-handled scoop. A small amount is left in to serve a very useful function as it is an excellent antacid and antiseptic. When the gourd is dried and cleaned it serves as a container for water that can be carried safely on a burro without losing a drop. It is also a rat-proof container for rice or beans or meal. Cut in half it becomes two bowls. Cut into pieces it becomes many saucers. Consider the calabash!"

A woman just preparing to bake some meal cakes over a charcoal fire caught Lorena's attention. *"Quitte um tiré portré ou, no?"* asked Lorena.

Reser laughingly urged the woman to consent, and Lorena hurried to the car for her camera. I went with her to get the candy and gifts we had brought along for the children.

I had just collected the various items in the car and Lorena was adjusting the lens hood on her camera when I saw a figure coming slowly and apparently unseeingly down the road in front of us. He was somewhat below medium height, coalblack and thin. Light knee-length pants, a wide-open faded blue shirt, a tattered straw hat were his attire. He walked as a man walks in his sleep, while his hands, moving machinelike, braided long narrow strands of sisal which trailed behind him like serpents at his heels.

"Look!" My whispered word was all Lorena needed. Her promise to Reser made way for an instinctive move. Stepping into the man's path she raised her camera and clicked the shutter. Something deep within him looked out at her. It was like the passing of a fading light vanishing into nothingness. She waited until he came nearer and photographed him again. Then he passed by, braiding the sisal without stopping.

Lorena came back to the car, and her hands shook as she proceeded to change the film.

"That," she said, "was terrific!"

"Add a zombi to your documentary," I told her.

"You think he was?"

"I'll ask Reser."

"Do you think you should?"

"Why not?"

"Zombis aren't supposed to be, are they?"

"Many people say they can't be," I answered.

"Whatever he was, I've got him black on white."

"You were lucky. Or were you?"

"What do you mean?" she said with a light laugh. "Are you getting superstitious?"

"No . . . but didn't someone tell us that here in Haiti the picture taker is worse off than the one whose picture is taken?"

"I'm not worried," she said with a toss of her head. "Do you really think he was a zombi? What was he doing with those long sisal strips?"

"They make hats out of them."

"Zombi or no zombi," she concluded, "this film goes into the crocodile case along with the rest of the loot. Lock the car."

I decided to have a talk with Reser about this. No one ever came to Haiti without hearing the word zombi, which Webster defines as a reanimated dead body. Were zombis only a myth? Did they stand in the same legendary relation to Haitians that banshees did to the Gaels, werewolves to the Anglo-Saxons and satyrs to the Greeks? Were they no more real than the erlking or the Lorelei or the thousand and one other demons and pixies with which romanticists have peopled the unseen world? Did imagination create them, and superstition give them life? The talk of zombis persisted, and no one ever wrote about Haiti without mentioning them. No one touched Voodoo without feeling their shadows. No one could believe in the *loa* without wondering about the living dead.

We walked slowly back to the group behind the house. The children showed their delight in the candy and gifts in a rippling murmur of Creole. Lorena won the favor of the women to such an extent that she not only took a whole series of pictures but also began to learn the fine art of cooking over a charcoal fire.

Reser said, "The *houngan,* Ti Cousin, will be here in a little while. Be ready with your questions. Here's the place to get the answers."

"I have one for you," I said.

"Shoot."

"Zombis."

He shrugged. "What about them?" he asked.

"That's the question," I replied. "What about them? I asked a businessman in Port-au-Prince. He said, 'Sure there are zombis in Haiti. You have them in America, too. There you call them psychopaths. They have illusions about being the reincarnation of Napoleon or Christophe or somebody. Some of them do nothing but walk. Some do nothing but work. Some do nothing. Zombis? What's a zombi? He's a man who is out of his mind.' "

"That's the extent of your research?" Reser asked cryptically.

"No," I told him. "Others had other ideas. A doctor told me that Voodoo priests have strange powers. They understand the use of drugs and herbs that can put a man in a state of suspended animation. He reminded me that here in Haiti people are not embalmed, that many times they are buried without a doctor's certificate of death. He thought it was entirely possible that a man could be drugged and buried and the whole thing so timed that the victim regained consciousness, say at the eerie hour of midnight. Standing next to him when he came to would be the man who had drugged him. 'Come,' says the man, 'I resurrected you. You belong to me.' "

"Why would a man want to do that?" Reser queried skeptically.

"So the zombi would work for him like a machine."

"Nonsense. Labor is not that expensive in Haiti."

"Maybe just to show his power."

"Whose power?"

"The priest's power. If he has a zombi on his plantation, don't you suppose that those who see the zombi are reminded of the mystical power of the *houngan?*"

"There are other ways of showing the power," Reser declared.

"Well, Stanley," I asked, "what is a zombi?"

He reflected a moment and said, "Your doctor informant was correct. It is possible that drugs are given by unscrupulous evildoers for revenge or some other personal motive. The drug causes a cataleptic state that is readily accepted for death. After burial the victim can be removed from the tomb the same night and revived enough to travel. From then on what happens is only conjecture."

"Have you ever encountered one of these zombi travelers?" I asked.

"In all my years in Haiti—just one. A true *houngan,* like Ti Cousin or any other reputable priest, will have nothing to do with these things. That is the work of charlatans. It always amazes me," he added, "how people from the States get excited about zombis. What goes on in America? There narcotics are used for healing and remedial purposes, but sometimes criminals use them for making addicts even out of school children. The wholesale use of drugs in the States is a great deal more sinister than here where the rare *houngan* turns some isolated wanderer into a servant."

He said no more, for his eyes were fixed on a tall commanding black figure approaching us with timeless step. He had appeared with shocking suddenness. A smile played on his lips, both hands were already extended in open welcome to the white man at my side.

2.

"MEN misunderstand Voodoo when they think of it only as sense perception. It is something intuitive and spiritual."

The voice was the voice of Reser, but the thoughts were those of old Ti Cousin. The strange white man was merely acting as interpreter for the even stranger black priest. The *houngan* sat regally on a straight-backed chair, his black hat squarely on his head, a hand on each knee. He was tall and gaunt, an age-less old man, vitally alert behind a masklike composure. His eyes stared at me as if they were turning the pages of my life and reading whatever they wished.

"It does not follow that the most intelligent or the most highly trained person is best qualified for spiritual experiences. What-ever limits a man's nature subjectively only retards it spir-itually." The setting sun cast high lights upon the *houngan's* solemn face. He was a symbol of quiet strength and secret con-templation. "If learning binds man to that which is physical, learning is of no use. If ignorance binds him, ignorance is bad. Voodoo is a process to loose man and lift him. Voodoo is an expression of interest in everything from the earth to eternity. Voodoo is an expression of faith."

Reser translated the words like a sensitized instrument. He sat in a rocker clasping his unlighted pipe between both hands

and speaking the words of Ti Cousin as if this were a well-re-
hearsed dramatic presentation. Outside the little screened-in
porch the people of the plantation walked like the passing of
time. A black boy lay listlessly in the crotch of the calabash
tree. A man who could not conceivably have known the mean-
ings of time or joy stood in the yard endlessly braiding strands
of sisal between his mechanized hands.

"Ti Cousin wants to know if you have any questions," Reser
announced, pressing his finger into the cold bowl of his pipe.

"What is the theory of possession?" I asked. "What is its purpose?"

Before I had finished my words were already transposed into
Creole, and the answers came so rapidly that I could not say
which were Reser's thoughts and which were Ti Cousin's. As
a matter of fact, it was impossible to avoid the feeling that the
two men were governed simultaneously by one active character.

"Possession goes back to the pythoness of the Greeks" was the
reply. "She was the mouthpiece of the gods. When she sat at
Delphi a vapor and a mist engulfed her. A vapor and a mist—
or the sound of drums. . . . The gods have their own designs.
Possession takes many forms. That is because there are many
kinds of spirits. It is the duty of the priest to know and to recog-
nize the good from the evil. We know when possession is true
and when it is not true."

"Tell him that possession reminds me of the baptism of the
Holy Spirit in some of our Holiness churches."

To this the *houngan* and Reser replied, "Every divine phenomenon must be a universal phenomenon. It cannot be confined to any one locality, though there seems to be localization
in the degree of the power. Where possession has been known

to occur frequently it would indicate that the elements necessary to possession are found there in greater abundance than elsewhere. What are called miracles happen best where they happen most. Voodoo has developed possession to an unusually high degree. The *veve* which the priest makes is a catalyst bringing about a synthesis of the spirit and the worshipers. It is this mystical act that starts the process of the spirit-man crystallization."

I had no way of knowing how much my able interpreter colored the words of the Voodoo patriarch. The force of argument flowed in an unbroken exposition of ideas completely harmonious. I heard possession by the *loa* compared to shamanism in Asia, to the spirit-dancers in China, to the Chao of Siam. This was "Voodoo talk" of a kind I had never expected to hear. I looked up in astonishment, trying to reconcile the words with the black priest and the lowly surroundings. What would Voodoo services be like on this plantation? Would we see things as amazing as the things I was hearing?

"Consider," my interpreter said, "how our people came to this land and how Voodoo was brought here. Contrast this with the way your religion came to your country. Our people were slaves. We were first oppressed, then isolated. But our spirits were never captive."

There were theological concepts startling and provocative. "Is it not difficult to say that there is one God and He is good when there is so much in the world that is evil? Is it not a problem to think of Him as the God of love when men hate one another as they do? There are lesser deities, intermediaries, some of whom are good and some bad. There is one Cosmic Reality, but there are many expressions. There are minor gods of earth and sea and sky."

"Ask Ti Cousin," I said, "what the moral and ethical standards of Voodoo are."

"They are the standards of the Catholic Church" came the
immediate reply. "But that is not all. Who can define what is
moral and what is ethical? The soul that is lost in the consciousness of the universe has its own standards."

The screened-in porch on a Haitian plantation became a class-
room. The easygoing, positive voice that spoke the Creole and
the rapid English voice that made the Creole intelligible to me
talked as familiarly about ancient philosophies and modern
thought as though this were a college seminar. Haiti, eighty-
per-cent illiterate; Voodoo, a despised religion; *houngans,* the
purported workers in black magic—all would have to be re-
evaluated in the light of this experience. I wondered whether
anyone who claimed that Voodoo gave its people nothing more
than a license to go crazy had ever sat in on such a discussion.

Frequently Reser punctuated his remarks with a delighted
"Oh-o!" or an enthusiastic *"Ai-yai-yai!"* as Ti Cousin coined a
phrase or presented a new idea.

"He says," Reser would exclaim, "that faith is a growing tree
and the blight and disease that strike it are unbelief and fear."

Occasionally proverbs came into the talk: A scalded cat is
afraid of cold water. . . . It is the empty calabash that makes
the most noise. . . . A strong wind uncovers the hen's behind.

Then there were humorous recollections. "There was once an
houngan who was called 'Butterfly.' One night at a service he
was making a *veve* on the ground, and out of the darkness two
butterflies came fluttering in. One lighted on his arm, the other
in the center of the *veve.* This was not the butterfly season! The
people chanted and danced and not until they had finished did
the butterflies go away. A Haitian attorney who had come to

scoff said, 'This is a mystery. In the face of a phenomenon like this, I take off my hat. Any man who can train butterflies is a stronger man than I!' "

And there were times of serious reflection. Reser said, "Every once in a while, the government and the church try to discourage Voodoo practices and confiscate Voodoo articles. In one of these purges the *houngan* Dorsema was caught and thrown into prison. A Catholic priest came to visit him. 'Dorsema,' said the priest, 'you are a wise man. Give up this charlatanism.' Dorsema answered, 'When you entered the priesthood, father, you felt you had a call to help people. I, too, have had a call.' 'But this Voodoo,' moaned the cleric, 'this kind of thing works only evil.' 'It heals people,' said Dorsema. 'It helps people to understand the working of the saints.' 'It is false!' cried the priest. Dorsema said, 'Let us put this to a test. If what I tell you is not true, you may leave me here in prison. If it is, see that I am released.' 'Fair enough,' said the priest. 'What is it?' Dorsema told him, 'While we were talking, father, there came to the post office a letter for you. The letter is this large. It has a black border. It tells of the death of your mother in France. Go and see!' The priest went to the post office, and there was the letter as predicted. Dorsema was released."

There were many hours like this on the plantation at Léogane. There were many days in which Reser and Ti Cousin had their private meetings and, I have no doubt, their solemn exchange of Voodoo secrets into which the uninitiated never enter. Voodoo is a fraternity and its solidarity is its hidden teaching. This no outsider has ever written about, and this Reser would no more have betrayed than would he have divulged his Masonic obligation. There is one sure way to learn about these secrets: that is, to become an initiate of the order, to take *kanzo* and to live the life.

3.

THEN one afternoon Reser said, "Ti Cousin is going to do you a great favor. He will take you into his private chapel."

Lorena and I walked with the old Voodoo seer across the plantation grounds. His movements were always dramatic. His unhurried stride, his straight bearing, the calm turn of his head and the fixed, lingering glance of his dark eyes were signs that he was consciously or unconsciously playing a part. On this occasion he carried in his hand a large brass key.

It was nearing sundown when we walked through the shaded yard, and I could not help but envy the black man for the sense of peace which he affirmed as he paused before a small plot of ground closed in by a wrought-iron fence. Within the grassy spot was a tomb—a stone tomb like a grotto.

"*Kay mwe*," he said, and his smile was one of resignation and trust. *Kay mwe*—my home.

He had built it for himself against the day of his death. His eyes lingered on it. I could almost imagine him walking through the iron gate into the darksome sepulcher and lying down, confident that the faith which he practiced would not forsake him.

Since fantastic tales about death exist throughout Haiti, I asked Reser about some of the customs.

"Sure there are some strange practices," he said, amused. "It is not unusual among some of the mountain folk, when preparing a body for burial, to scatter handfuls of tiny sesame seeds all over the corpse and in the coffin. In the event an evil spirit should try to take the body he would first have to find and remove every one of the seeds. This would be so annoying he would give up in disgust. Another humorous practice is that of wrapping a piece of thread around a needle with a broken eye and placing it carefully on the breast of the departed. Then the devil will become so frustrated trying to thread the needle he'll probably curse a few times and go his nefarious way."

"But what about the death of an *houngan?*" I asked.

"Immediately after a *mambo* or an *houngan* dies," he explained, "a prominent associate priest is called upon to perform the obligatory service of *dessounin.* The priest, with one or two indispensable assistants, sends everyone out of the room, even the members of the family. Sheets are pinned up to insure absolute privacy. The deceased is stood upright. Just what happens then is a ritual secret, but I can tell you that, after the *veve* of the guardian spirit has been made and the usual prayers and invocations have been solemnly intoned, the *maitre tete,* the personal *loa,* is invoked into the *govi.* This sacred jar is then carefully sealed and the spirit may be consulted in time of need. There is nothing to distinguish the burial of an *houngan* from that of any other prominent person."

I urged him to tell me more about the *maitre tete,* for I had heard that locks of hair and fingernails were put into the *govi* first and that these lured the spirit inside.

Reser's reply was curt. "To divulge what I actually know about the ritual would be a breach of confidence."

This settled it for the moment, for Ti Cousin was leading us to his chapel, the Maison Saint Jacques. With the big brass key he unlocked the weathered door and led us in.

It was dark and chilly inside, but the afternoon light came in through the small windows sufficiently to reveal a beautifully decorated altar. This was the *Pe*, the great altar of the inner room. Ti Cousin, silent as a painted figure, stood by while Reser pointed out several articles which were new to us. There were a number of *pierre tonner*, thunder stones, polished black, very much like the *pierre loa*. These stones, Reser explained, had fallen out of space during a storm. He told us that one such stone had been given to him through the guidance of a *loa* after a heavy rain. He had been carrying a cane that day and when he put it down in a small puddle of water a violent shaking was felt. Looking down he saw the *pierre tonner*.

The central object on the *Pe* was a crucifix surrounded by lithographs of Catholic saints. What corresponded to the votive light in Catholicism was a bowl of sweet oil in which floated wicks made of cotton mesh rolled and fixed with pitch pine. The basin which Catholic priests use in the lavabo was here a calabash bowl with water. Mother Church's patens were here earthen dishes; her chalices, cups and glasses; her amphoras, bottles of wine, liqueur and rum. The emblem of the priestly office on this *hounfort* altar was the *asson* with its network of beads and sections of snake vertebrae. In place of a thurible I saw a mortar in which sweet-smelling spices had been stirred. Instead of sacramental wafers I saw cakes of meal, rice, pineapple, bananas and ears of corn—also an egg, the eternal symbol of fertility and life.

A complex assortment of cups, *govis*, conches, artificial flowers, porcelain bowls, bottles of cologne all found a place. Evidently articles and elements were here for every ministration. Ti Cousin was well equipped for the performance of services of healing, sacrifice, expiation or praise.

But my attention was held by something black, a small cloth effigy without face or features. To me it meant only one thing— a *wanga*—and here in this darkening chapel it cast a spell of my own making, perhaps, but nonetheless real. I glanced inquiringly at Reser. He was occupied describing various items to Lorena with his usual thoroughness. I looked at Ti Cousin, towering at my side. His eyes distended, then he smiled and motioned to me to follow him.

I went with him to the rear of the chapel where he opened a door and asked me to go in. This room, I was sure, had nothing to do with *wangas* or black magic. It might well have been a sleeping room for an honored guest. The bedspread was of fine silk and the pillow cases were attractively embroidered. A washstand held a basin with water, white towels and soap, a comb, brush and various powders and perfumes. Above a small altar on which were both freshly cut and artificial flowers was an expensive lithograph of the jewel-bedecked Mater Dolorosa.

Ti Cousin was pleased when I expressed my admiration. His reply was gentle. He said, "Erzilie Freda."

He closed the door. With simple piety he took a bottle and sprinkled cologne on the little altar, then stood there, lifting a hand as if to sign himself with the cross. With hands joined he meditated. *"M' apé rele, Gran Erzilie."* (I call upon you, noble Erzilie.)

This was the room of Erzilie Freda, the *loa* who was identified with the Virgin. The room was clean, as she was clean, and Ti Cousin prayed that his thoughts might be pure, as Erzi-

lie's are pure. It was she whom Reser had graphically described
to me when he said, "The first African slaves seeing the picture
of the Mater Dolorosa said, 'She loves beautiful things. She is
Erzilie.'"

This was a spiritual bridal suite into which no mortal woman
ever came. A priest may have many wives or no wife, he may
have many loves or few, but he always has Erzilie. She is
wealthy and beautiful, she can be voluptuous and seductive, her
heart knows sadness and sorrow, and her soul is full of joy and
compassion for all men. When a man marries he thinks of
Erzilie, for she is the example of perfect womanhood. Before a
child is born it is well to bring her an offering. It is good to
have Erzilie as an unseen but never unknown godmother.
When Erzilie calls, a good man will leave those he loves, however dearly, and follow her voice. On Erzilie's days, which are
Tuesday and Thursday, he will go to her room and feel the
tender embrace of her presence. Erzilie is man's highest passion
and delight, and her favorite sacrifice is a pair of white hens or
white pigeons.

As I watched Ti Cousin stand solemnly at Erzilie's altar, I
thought of the sequestered monks in the Catholic faith as I had
seen them transfixed and motionless before the Virgin's statue.
Often they knelt or prostrated themselves at her feet. For hours
they gazed into her face. "They are in love," an abbot once told
me, "in love with a Woman. Their lives are lost in love for
Her."

Reluctantly Ti Cousin drew away from his act of consecra-
tion. He turned to me. Did I not want to show my respect to
Erzilie? Was I not moved to honor her? Reverently I sprinkled
cologne on the altar and then stood before the picture of the

saintly Mother, trying to think the thoughts of Ti Cousin while feeling a greater nearness to his faith.

We returned to the chapel where Reser was favoring Lorena with an intensive course in Voodoo lore. His voice was buoyant, for he wanted us to know that Voodoo was not as gloomy as some of the crude furnishings of the altar might suggest. He held up a strand of beads and explained that each color represented a different *loa*. Then he draped the beads around Lorena's neck saying that she would be an excellent *hounsi*. He was most pleased that Ti Cousin had taken special interest in me and had shown me Erzilie's room.

"Erzilie," said Reser, "is indescribable. I went to one of her services one night. All of the women were dressed in silks and satins and heavily perfumed. *Ai-yai-yai!* They all wanted to be as lovely as Erzilie. The service was held in a private home. I had been up so late the night before that I was worn out before the ceremony was over. The lady of the house said there was a guest room for me. I went in and immediately fell asleep. When I woke up in the morning and put my feet on the floor I jumped. The bottom of my feet were lacerated with tiny wounds and scratches. When a servant brought in the morning coffee I said, 'Look at my feet! What kind of mice shared this room with me?' She laughed and called her mistress who asked me to get up and go to the window. 'There,' she said, 'are the mice!' The courtyard was made of crushed gravel. Then she told me about thirty minutes after I retired the tempo of the singing changed. She said, 'You got up out of bed and danced possessed of Erzilie out there in the yard. You didn't say anything to anybody, but when the long dance was over you saluted, said good night and went back to sleep.' It was Erzilie's night."

Ti Cousin spread his large black hands over the altar. He selected a bottle that stood near the little black cloth object. The *houngan* proceeded to remove the cork from the bottle.

Reser watching him said, "Whatever he asks you to do, don't refuse him."

The bottle contained a yellowish liquid into which some herbs had been stuffed. Ti Cousin filled an altar glass with this questionable brew and handed it to Reser. Reser took it saying, "He wants us to have a drink of fellowship." Then he saluted Ti Cousin with the glass and drank it down.

The *houngan* next poured out a glassful for me. I took it and saluted him, then raised the glass to Reser and said, "For the sake of research!"

"It's the elixir of life!" was the jovial reply.

It may have been the elixir of life, but I thought it was going to kill me for sure. My throat felt as if it were having its *kanzo.* I was burning inside.

I felt sorry for Lorena when old Ti Cousin handed her a glassful, but she drank it like a man.

The moments immediately following this drink of fellowship were vague. I remember catching sight of one of Ti Cousin's rare smiles that filled the hollows of his face and brought him nearer to a person of our world. I remember how his black hand pressed the corncob cork into place. He eyed the contents and set the bottle back on the altar next to the red earthen jars and the white bowls and the black object that I called a *wanga.* I remember that he picked up the *asson* as if to show us its workmanship and let us hear its haunting sound. There was also the locking of the door with the big brass key and the walk past the tomb, but I remember best Reser's remark as we jolted merrily in our *oto* over the rough road leading back to Port-au-

Prince. He said, "I am glad you two were such good sports. Ti Cousin likes you and he wants us back for the big service of the year. Christmas Eve. It's a great honor that he has invited you, don't you think? Can you make it?"

"We wouldn't miss it for the world!" we said in unison.

"Stanley," I added, "I have never tasted canned heat or anti-freeze, but it can't be any worse than the stuff we had out of that bottle."

He replied, "Maybe so. But don't you feel good?"

We all felt wonderful.

4·

ON DECEMBER 24 we rented a *ligne,* called for Reser at the Chez Pauline and set out once more for the *houngan's* habitation. At a thatch-roofed roadside stand near Carrefour where Stanley was well-known we stopped to buy some extra fine *tablettes noix,* a sort of praline made of cashew nuts and brown sugar. We also had gifts in the car for the children and a bottle of Bacardi rum for our friend, Ti Cousin.

Christmas was in the air, and there was nothing incongruous about the fact that we alternately sang the old-time carols and Voodoo songs as we drove along the lovely sun-bathed countryside. Who has ever seen a Haitian highway without thinking of Bethlehem? The women on their burros and the walking men are tableaux of the Mary and Joseph story. The vendors with their packs walking with steady, rhythmic step are now the Magi. The men in the fields are the shepherds, the women and the children the pilgrims, and every lowly straw-thatched dwelling is a manger.

The plantation houses had been scoured for the holiday and were festive with flowers and festooning. I insisted that old Ti Cousin knew in advance the hour of our arrival, for we were greeted with small cups of hot, black coffee and deliciously roasted peanuts. All was ready and waiting, having been brought that very moment from the wattle-walled kitchen.

"He also wants you to have some coconut milk," Reser said, and Ti Cousin turned to a young boy who stood eagerly at the base of a towering palm. At the old man's command, the boy sped up the lofty trunk with the ease and grace of a monkey. Soon he was tossing down coconuts for our party. A man with a machete in his skilled hands deftly squared off the outer husk, then cut a hole in the shell which permitted us to drink.

As we sat on the back porch of the *houngan's* home, a place so small that we had to sit cozily close together, the conversation again turned to Voodoo. Once more Ti Cousin was the inform-ant and Reser the interpreter. I learned how closely, from every point of view, Voodoo is related to the whole broad run of Catholic teaching. The *loa,* as we had already seen, are the saints. The "island below the sea" is purgatory. *Paquets* are like Catholic charms and amulets. The *houngan's* temple cere-monies are comparable to the Mass, his services for the departed like the church's prayers for the dead. The obligations he places upon his people are similar to penances, and the secrets of the people are their confessions told to him in confidence. This concept of Voodooism was vastly different from the claim that it is cannibalism and that its drumheads are human skins.

As I looked out over the grounds realizing that hidden away among the thick green growths were many Voodoo shrines I wondered again what would be revealed to us at this Christ-mastide.

In the plantation yard a large group was assembling in anti-
cipation of the sacred night. There was much activity among
the women who worked feverishly with last-minute preparations over the charcoal fires. Children stood around sucking at
sticks of sugar cane and eating white strips of coconut. Girls
and young men in holiday mood and in gala attire loitered in
small groups chattering gaily. There were a few seemingly
poor and neglected bystanders, but they all had one claim in
common: Ti Cousin was their mighty leader who had power
over them, body and soul. They belonged to him as willing
votaries, believing him the possessor of supernatural authority
and wisdom. He was their priest, their archbishop, their Pope.

A woman sorting yams near the calabash tree began a happy
little song to the saints. Reser voiced a joyous *"Ai-yai-yai"* and
joined in the singing which soon filled the yard. The *houngan,*
pleased with the bottle which we had brought as a gift, picked
it up and suggested it was high time for a drink of fellowship.

It was at sundown, after we had tasted deeply of the rum, that I
became conscious of a more intoxicating influence—the steady
staccato beat of the drums booming out a Nago rhythm, 123456,
123456, 123456789. Over and over it rolled in like the tide of
the sea. The people in the yard began to wander in the direction
of the sound. Ti Cousin's moist eyes roved over us. When
they rested upon me I felt again an indescribable return to
some previous encounter long before I ever came to Haiti.
Far behind the first faint hint of Voodoo in my consciousness
I felt that I had been here in this same scene long ages ago. I
caught Ti Cousin's unwavering gaze.

Reser was speaking. "Ti Cousin wonders what you are
thinking."

"I was thinking," I said, and the words were like someone speaking for me, "I was just thinking of a talk I gave to a group of Negro students in a southern school back in the States. I said to them, 'It is as easy for me to believe in a pre-existence as in a life to come. Who is to say we have not lived before?' That night a young man spoke up and said, 'And would you say, sir, that in that life before you were also white?' "

The eyes of the old priest were like dark stars to which my own eyes gave the light. The watery film, like tears of compassion behind which the dark pigment mysteriously hovered, reminded me of the "island beneath the sea," where the dead still live and the *loa* speak.

He smiled and his eyes half closed. He spoke so quietly that not even Reser discerned what he was saying. Folding his heavily veined hands the *houngan* sat for a long time as if in prayer. Never did the steady rumble of the drums creep more hauntingly into my heart; never did their throb and beat weave with greater intensity into every fiber of my being than on this night. I had always had the power to listen to them critically, as one listens to a theatrical performance. For the first time I felt insecure. For the first time I wished they would stop.

Lorena's voice came to me with a shock. "Look! Isn't that pretty!"

Her words brought me back to reality. She was standing in the doorway gazing out across the plantation. I went over and stood beside her in the deepening shadows. All along the pathway on the other side of the road small candles were twinkling close to the ground. Black, moving forms were pressing candles into the earth on each side of the dirt path about three feet apart. A carpet of light was unfolding to the sound of the drums. Then all was silent. The candles burned fitfully. The evening wind murmured through the fields of sugar cane. The first star appeared above the distant hills.

The thought of Christmas Eve returned. Voodoo drew nearer to Christianity. The plantation custom of lighting candles reflected a universal symbolism. Softly the drums began again. They had a reassuring tone. I was ready once more to enter into the spirit of a people's faith.

Ti Cousin uncoiled his long body from the chair. Just inside the door was a large bronze portrait bust, a perfect image of him. From it he took his black hat, which had been set on the sculptured piece, put it on his head and beckoned to us to follow him. It had grown quite dark now. The air was cool. The soft breeze fanned the low-flaming candles as we walked between the rows. Near by on both sides stood the plantation workers and neighbors who had come for the service. Eighty or a hundred men and women watched the deliberate figure of the *houngan* as he led us on. Many of them greeted Reser with a warm *"Bonsoir."*

"The service will be held in the *hounfort*," Reser explained.

We could see the outline of the *hounfort* in the distance. It was a chapel attached to the *tonnelle*. Near it small groups of worshipers waited. Here, too, a number of turkeys and chickens were tied. Reser pointed to these captives as much as to say, Plenty of sacrifices!

We went into the *tonnelle* where the three drummers welcomed Ti Cousin with a spurt of added animation in their skillful handling of the Nago beat. The *houngan* smiled and nodded his approval. The people waited, all of them in a happy mood, all unhurried and seemingly unconcerned whether the service should begin now or later. It was all up to Ti Cousin, and whatever he willed was right.

He raised a hand to us and led us out as a few men with white scarves around their heads came in. A woman with a naked child in her arms also entered, followed by other women and several small children. Reser relayed Ti Cousin's message to us.

"We're going to eat. A special meal has been prepared."

"When does the service start?" Lorena asked.

"There's no rush," Reser answered.

We were taken to a cozy, well-built house not far from the *tonnelle* where a woman held open the door for our host. A large table had been set for us and two women were waiting to serve us, but the object that caught our attention was a shining, up-to-date gas refrigerator at one end of the room! This might have been a scene in a modern country home anywhere in the States. The fresh vegetables, jellies, generous servings of salad and colorful fruit were like a Sunday farm dinner.

But the *pièce de résistance* was the deliciously prepared meat of young goat that had been selected especially for us. It was flavorfully roasted, brown and succulent. Ti Cousin enjoyed seeing us eat, though he ate sparingly, and Reser had the fun of playing a practical joke on me. He dared me to follow his example in eating a whole *piment* pepper. I did and found my throat and stomach burning with as fierce a fire as was ever kindled in any ceremonial pit. I tried to quench it with ice water and wine and finally got up in agony to walk off the torture on the dark plantation grounds.

I strode down the path where the candles were burning low and made my way to the car, where I curled up for a few minutes, suffering the pangs of the damned. The pain was eased not a bit by the undying chatter of the savage drums. My mouth felt as though it had been swabbed out with a blowtorch, but the humor of the thing finally caught up with me. I wiped the tears from my eyes and went back to the house. Reser apologized and said that just for penance he would eat three of the *piment* peppers. This he did without batting an eye and then remarked, "Only we Haitians know how to eat these things." Lorena nibbled at one. I could see by the look on her face that she likewise could never fill this qualification for becoming a citizen of the Enchanted Isle.

It was a deliberate meal, lasting nearly an hour and a half. When we returned to the *tonnelle* the number of worshipers had doubled. This time Ti Cousin wearing a white turban that made him look toweringly tall led us through the crowd, and the eyes of the people were on him alone. They took it for granted that we would not be here except for his invitation and they greeted Reser almost as if he were Ti Cousin's *la place*. Maybe he was.

Two women lifted up varicolored silk flags when the *houngan* approached the door of the *hounfort*. Ti Cousin entered followed by Reser, Lorena and me. The scene that greeted us was one I had been anticipating ever since I first heard of Voodoo in some forgotten yesterday. I had always imagined that Voodoo was an intimate, clandestine gathering held in secret in a long, narrow, windowless room. I had always envisioned rows of staring, superstitious faces gazing at their priest in a reverence bordering on fear. I had pictured some of the worshipers being unable to see the master or bear his nearness without trembling or signs of emotion. I had expected that some would make the sign of the cross or kiss their thumbs or press their hands upon their breasts. All this now came into view, a living scene vividly painted on the canvas of my mind.

The people crowding the chairs and benches along the dark, stone walls were the seekers. Ti Cousin was the one who had found truth. They were the servants, he their master. They were the laity, he their priest before whose eyes they saw themselves in all their abjection and need and in whose presence they were stripped bare of secrets and sins. They looked at him wonderingly in fear and love.

The rectangular room about ten by thirty feet with its somewhat high, flat ceiling was lighted by candles and several lamps. At the end of the room opposite the entrance stood an altar table. On it were the conventional furnishings together with several bottles of rum.

Chairs had been reserved near this altar for us. Ti Cousin asked us to be seated while he stood at the altar murmuring prayers and occasionally touching several of the articles. I noticed a basin filled with water and asked Reser about this. He said it was for Damballa and Agué. Meanwhile the drummers came in from the *tonnelle* and took places opposite us. Then people began jamming the doorway.

My prevision of Voodoo returned and was justified by this scene: the stifling air, the smell of rum, the scent of burning candles, the sight of several men smoking cigarettes, mothers holding naked babies on their knees, and the turbaned *houngan* standing tall and straight. This was the scene we had been waiting for. We were out of the world we knew and behind the scenes at last. Reser was at perfect ease. He sat with his hands folded in his lap like a man safely at home in his most comfortable chair. His contention that a Voodoo service is unhurried was never truer than on this Christmas Eve. It seemed that Ti Cousin would remain at the altar forever. The long moments were counted off by the restless movement of a child, the clearing of a throat, a whisper in Creole, the faraway barking of a dog, voices on the plantation grounds, the echoing cry of a night bird.

Finally the *houngan* turned from the altar. His countenance was the semblance of perfect repose, though his eyes roved over the worshipers, touching us and then lifting for a moment toward heaven. He held the *asson* in his right hand. He raised it and began the *action de grace,* the unvarying ritual of prayers, hymns and a litany of the saints and the *loa.* Legba, the opener-of-the-gate and the shower-of-the-way, was saluted. The rattle of the *asson,* the low chant of the drums, the softly accented beat of the *ogan* were as tender as a lullaby.

Creole words mingled with *langage.* Reser, the perfect annunciator, synchronized his commentary with Ti Cousin's lines in whispered phrases. *"Mettons nous dans le presence de Dieu. . . .* Let us put ourselves in the presence of God. Now three Our Fathers and three Hail Marys. What you are hearing now is a *cantique.* Isn't it beautiful? Think of it! They call these people ignorant and illiterate. Listen to them! They know these rituals backward and forward. What's more, they know the symbolism behind all this. They know how to make contact."

Closing his eyes, he joined the voices. *"Venez, mon Dieu, venez, venez, mon doux Sauveur. . . .* Come, my Lord, come, come, my gentle Saviour. . . . *Venez regner en moi au contre de mon coeur. . . .* Come, take thy place near to my heart. . . . *Venez, mon Dieu, venez. . . .* Come, my Lord, come. . . ."

On and on it went, Catholic saints and Voodoo *loa,* signs of
the cross and Voodoo signs blending and interweaving with the
incessant rattle of the *asson.*

"In the name of the Father and of the Son and of the Holy
Ghost. *Relé Grand-Pere, Eternel, diore-é.* . . . Call great Father
eternal. *Relé Grand-Pere Eternel dior docrois agorié.*" Reser
explained that *docrois agorié* was *langage* and could not be
translated. *"Relé Grand-Pere Eternal . . . si nous lan main bon
Dieu . . .* if we are in the hands of God . . . *Oh, Seigneur . . .* Oh,
Lord."

The chant was repeated for the Virgin and the Saints. I
caught the names of all the old familiar ones: Jacques, Peter,
Nicolas, Joseph, Luc, Philippe, Catherine, Lucie. . . . I heard
the roster of the *mystère,* many of whom sounded like old
friends: Damballa Wedo, Ogoun Ferreille, Legba, Agué Woyo,
Erzilie, Petro, Gran Siligbo, Mait Carrefour, Smibi d'leau. And
many new ones: Mait Agasu, Loco Atissou, Agaou Tonnerre,
Azaca Mede, Maitresse La Sirene, Gran Dangny, Gran Aluba.

How many *loa?* How many saints? Who could tell? Only
the timeless black priest knew them all. Only the incredible
white man at my side did not run out of names. The eyes of
the two men often met when, between the different classes
of *loa,* they would chant together, *"Zo—Lissadolé—Zo!"* Words
that had meaning only to the gods.

In these moments the true devotion of the people could not
be questioned. The kneeling *hounsi* erased from my mind all
question that they were less sincere than acolytes in any
church or helpers in any service. What was religion's function?
Who was to say that one form of incantation was better or worse
than another? It all depended upon how a man wished to look

at it. He could say that Voodoo was stupidity and superstition, black magic and hocus-pocus; or he could look upon it as a profound and worshipful impulse on the part of a believing people.

I wished that everyone who said his prayers in cathedrals and chapels, and everyone who chanted his offices in the sumptuous surroundings of manse or rectory could have been in this unpretentious *hounfort,* and that everyone could have felt the reciprocal power that played between the unseen saints and the worshipers. I wished, too, that he might have felt the supersensitivity and priestly majesty with which the aged *houngan* poured the libation to the cardinal points of the universe. His face in the candles' glow was black as night, but his presence was illumined.

He extended his hands to Reser. The white man rose and shook hands with the priest vigorously three times with wrists crossed, then took the urn, blessed the four corners of the *hounfort* and returned to the altar where he stood quietly for a time.

Ti Cousin signalled to someone in the doorway. The people who crowded this passage moved aside letting in a sudden welcome gust of air. A man entered bearing a galvanized tub which he set in the center of the room. The worshipers registered expectancy and watchful waiting as the drummers started a *Jan Valo* rhythm: 1-2, 1-2, 1-**2**-3-4-5. The *houngan* watched through half-closed eyes as a woman came in clasping a small armful of green leaves.

"You are very lucky," Reser confided. "This is a service which few outsiders ever see. Tonight the children will be made immune against disease, and health and protection will be assured them for the coming year."

I tried to relate this to the Christmas story. Perhaps there was a distant connection, since supposedly on this night long ago Jesus had been born to sanctify for all time the birth of children everywhere. His nativity, in a place more lowly than this *houn-fort,* was being commemorated in its own special way by these Voodoo-Christians. They joined the *houngan* in a chant as the woman tucked the leaves together into tiny packs and placed them in symmetrical fashion in the tub.

When she had finished another woman entered bringing handfuls of herbs. These she arranged in the tub with special care. Then in unhurried succession a procession of women appeared, each one bringing leaves, herbs, aromatic roots and medicinal grasses which, under the close scrutiny of Ti Cousin, were placed in proper order in the tub.

"Never have I seen such a variety," Reser observed aloud. "There must be forty or fifty different kinds. These things have been collected far off in the hills and represent some of the rarest and most essential medicinal plants. Ti Cousin is an expert herbalist."

The breaking and assorting of these offerings filled the room with an aromatic scent. The mingled poignant odors rose like incense. A young man now poured water over the herbs and the seven *hounsi* began a dance around the tub intended, no doubt, to sanctify the elements and to set the gods in motion. The drums were the rumble of thunder, and the sensation of watching the encircling figures brought to mind the hidden symbolism which Reser and I had often talked about in relation to the Voodoo dance. Was it possible that the *hounsi* represented the seven ancient planets in their circle dance? Was the tub, now bearing the remedial power of the earth, a symbol of the

Sun or God? If so, Reser was right in his contention that Voodoo was rooted in great antiquity, for the planetary dance was as old as time. Voodoo also reached forward. Among the American Shakers the circle dance had been known and practiced, and on this Christmas Eve among holiness groups in America there would be the turning movement of the hallelujah march invoking the baptism of the Holy Ghost.

At Ti Cousin's signal the dancing stopped. The drums started a *Mahi* (Dahomey) rhythm and five women fell to their knees around the tub. They seized the wet herbs between the palms of their hands and began a threshing motion, intent on grinding the aromatic stuff into a thin, mashy substance. This began with feverish intensity, with singing and shouts of delight like the operation of a *coumbite*. Only now it was religious fervor whipped up by the cavernous roar of the drums and the shriek of the *ogan*. The syncopated beats buried themselves in our minds: 1-2-**3**-4-5-6; 1-2-**3**-4-5-6; 1-2-**3**; 1-2-**3**; 1-2-**3**-4-5-6. All the while the metallic voice of the *houngan* rose and fell in a wailing dirge while he rattled the *asson*.

One of the women at the tub became possessed. A *loa* entered her head strongly. She spun about the room. She spoke *langage* while the worshipers applauded by beating their knees with their hands. She pirouetted wildly, striking some of the spectators with her body and almost falling into the tub. One of the *hounsi* took her place in the circle of women who continued to knead and roll and grind the herbs between their hands.

While the possessed woman was madly dancing, the *loa* seized another worker at the tub. This one rocked with laughter, flung up her stained hands and sent a spatter of green over us. She rose to her feet, eyes half-closed, and spoke in the "unknown tongue." We watched her move toward us with outstretched arms, and in a moment her twitching fingers seized Lorena by the shoulders. I turned to Reser for a cue, inquiring with a glance whether this was part of what one might expect. He nodded and smiled.

"Why not?" he said with a shrug. "You've been at Pentecostal services, haven't you?"

I had been to many of them. This was Pentecostal Voodoo. No phrase described it better. Still I was worried about Lorena. She was now down on her knees, and the "*loa*" stood over her triumphant.

I looked again. Lorena was at the tub grinding the wet leaves between the palms of her hands, unpossessed but certainly entering into the spirit of the affair!

Then a third woman in a strong state of possession grabbed me. I said, "Just a moment!" took off my wrist watch and rolled up my sleeves, got down on my knees and squeezed in between two women at the tub. The green, slimy water felt wonderfully cool to the touch, and the syncopated tangle of the drums united all of us into an operating mechanism smooth as a machine. The woman next to me laughed hilariously as Lorena and I took a tip from her and washed our arms and faces with the scented water, leaving some green leaves sticking in our hair. Someone tossed a towel to us, and we hurriedly dabbed our faces. Then the towel was passed around so that the rest of the perspiring workers could wipe their faces and necks and keep the sweat from dripping into the sacred tub.

Out of the corner of my eye I saw a mother holding her small child by the finger tips and the boy was already catching the rhythm of the drums in his shiny black body. The swaying,

circling women in possession reeled and chanted. The *houngan*
swung his *asson* in symmetrical motions and the *ogantier* beat
together his pieces of steel. The floor shook. The air was alive
with sounds and smells. Voodoo was many things. It was also
an escape. And why not? Just now there was no other world,
no other home, no other faith. All were concentrated within
these four confining walls. There were no problems to be solved,
no tomorrows to be faced, no questions to be asked or answered,
no one to please or displease, no thought, care or responsibility.
Whatever a man might do in that moment would be right.
The world was his. Time and eternity were one. I threshed
the wet shreds of herbs between my palms, dipped into the
tub for a new handful, dropped them back, dipped up more,
mumbled the chant and felt like a king.

Behind me Reser applauded us with his characteristic *"Ai-
yai-yai!"* It was his way of saying *Bon, Bon!* You two are really
entering into the spirit of this!

We were. Lorena was scraping the bottom of the tub for the
last elusive scraps of green which still needed to be pulverized.
We breathed in the dizzying odor. We swayed with the drums.
We leaned back while a man poured more water into the tub.
The concoction was taking on the consistency and appearance
of green-pea soup. Many hands had gone into it and nearly
two hours had been consumed in its preparation, but there came
a time when the *houngan's* inspection called it good, and the *loa*
were satisfied.

We got up from our cramped positions and staggered to our
chairs. Ti Cousin looked at us and smiled. I liked him for that.
It also gave me license to start picking some of the wet green
leaves out of Lorena's hair.

5.

DURING the lull in the service Ti Cousin went
into an adjoining room, and we got up and stretched our legs.
A few men and women came over to talk with Reser and to
shake hands with us. Our Creole phrases pleased them, and I
vowed that when next I came to Haiti I would have learned the
language. Even the slightest attempt to converse with them in
their own tongue was an open sesame into their affections.
Lorena won them over when she said, *"Bon Noel! M'amuser
'm' en apil."* (Merry Christmas! I enjoy this very much.) But
to my question—*"Qui ca kap arive ensuite?"* (What happens
now?)—there was no reply. They looked at Reser as if to indicate that he knew better than they.

"Spirits or watchers or *loa*," he said, "whatever you wish to
call them, are powers and forces that rule our lives. This is the
time of the year to bless amulets and *gardes* according to ancient
wisdom, and these are the hours in which herbs play their most
important part according to esoteric knowledge. There is a
hidden teaching in Catholicism that traces epidemics and
plagues to the influence of the Unseen, and it proposes to ward
off this influence with magical powers, whether it calls these
powers magical or not. Its entire ritual is built on the idea that
discarnate spirits exist and must be appeased and controlled."

"So again there is a connection between this service and what
Catholicism teaches?" I asked.

"Why, certainly! There is nothing in the teaching of the
church that conflicts with Voodoo!"

"Will many of these people be going to the Catholic services tomorrow—on Christmas Day?"

"Why not? If they can get to a service they will surely go. Voodooists cannot imagine a double set of gods or a double set of truths. As far as they are concerned, Catholicism helps to explain Voodoo to them and gives it dignity. Voodoo helps to explain Catholicism and gives it meaning."

He repeated in Creole much of this to those who stood with us during this *entr'act* in the *hounfort*. They marveled at his wisdom and agreed.

"These people," he said with emphasis, "are not bireligious. They see all religion as *one*. And that is a good deal more than can be said of many of your so-called educated theologians and denominational-minded churchgoers. Every miracle, every act, every thaumaturgic ritual is simply an additional credential of the power of faith. If your Penitentes back in the States can demonstrate that there is no pain in flagellation, the *loa* can demonstrate it, too. If the Catholic saints can demonstrate the power of the bleeding heart, so can the Voodoo *mystère*. If there are Christian stigmatists, there are also other stigmatists, for the phenomenon is not limited to any sect or group. The thousand and one miraculous and seemingly bizarre evidences that God works in mysterious ways, as evidenced by Catholic teaching, are all verified by Voodoo. Away with your monopoly on things of the Spirit! Away with your religious exclusiveness! Away with this talk about many faiths! All is one and One is All!"

He poured himself a glass of rum from the altar and the people were pleased. Quietly he went on, "You ask about the relationship of Voodoo and the Church. There has, of course,

been a continual campaign against Voodoo. Why not? From
an institutionalized point of view, that has to be done. The
curse of Christianity is its institutionalization. That's the disease
that eats up its vitality. That's the true heresy."

He paused to translate his comments for his Haitian listeners,
then resumed. "The Church sometimes refuses to baptize babies
until the parents promise to renounce their Voodoo connection.
Some under pressure and persuasion agree to all this, but after
a lapse of time, especially after they have had a siege of bad luck
or sickness, they return to implore the *loa*. Or if they have a run
of good luck, they return to praise the *loa*."

"The priests know this?" I asked.

"Certainly! Why shouldn't they? And every priest ought to
know that in every religion we find the same primitive thought
and impulse if only we have the honesty and the daring to look
for it. These people greatly respect the Catholic priests. Only,
many of them are smarter in religious understanding than the
priests are, and they know it. Out in Croix des Bouquets the
people loved a certain priest because he bawled the hell out of
them. 'This priest is certainly sincere,' they said." When he
told this to the group in Creole they howled with laughter.

"Always remember this," Reser warned, "remember this
night. This gathering right here. This is Haiti. This is the
spirit of Voodoo. A friendly, fraternal spirit which you don't
find anywhere else. These are your so-called despised blacks.
I'll take them any time. When the Big Book is opened and all
the evidence is in I think we'll find that the whites have more
to answer for than do the blacks. At least they never had an
Inquisition, a Buchenwald or a Hiroshima." He was asked to
repeat what he had said and he added a story which caused a

great hush to fall over his listeners. They remained with eyes fixed on him as he interpreted it for us.

"It happened on a Christmas Eve several years ago. I was at a dinner much like the one we enjoyed tonight with Ti Cousin. Christmas Eve was on a Thursday that year. Thursday is Erzilie's day, and when rum was served at the table I raised my glass and said, 'Erzilie, this is your day and it is also Christmas Eve. Tonight two faiths blend into one. Tonight let me know thy truth. Erzilie, I don't drink on your day, but tonight I will and whatever I drink I drink to you. Do with me as you will.'" Then he dramatized how the rum glasses were filled and how he lifted his to his lips and drank.

"That was a dinner!" he recalled. "Barbecued steer, duck, pig, guinea hen, fruits and candies from North Africa. At the stroke of midnight when the meal was reaching its climax I heard a voice calling to me. I heard Erzilie. I excused myself while the guests complained that I should stay. The voice was stronger. It asked me to go into a deserted Voodoo chapel, which I did. I stayed there for an hour in prayer. I talked to Erzilie and then, do you know what she inspired me to do? She made me stand before that little altar and sing, 'O holy night! the stars are brightly shining, It is the night of the dear Saviour's birth.' There was no priest there, neither Catholic nor Voodoo. I was alone with those invisible ones who watch over our island and our lives. In that chapel I felt more of the real spirit of Christmas than I had ever experienced before. Catholicism is the white man's Voodoo. Voodoo is the black man's Catholicism. There is no difference. There is only one Great Unknowable—the *Gran Mait!*"

6.

ONCE more the drums were beating.

We seated ourselves near the altar with its flickering lamps burning in their bowls of oil. Around us in the solid oblong room the worshipers crowded into benches against the walls. Once more I reminded myself that this was Christmas Eve.

Presently a tremor passed through the people as if they had heard something which we did not hear. Eyes turned to the doorway. Ti Cousin stood at the end of the room holding a sword in his gnarled black hands. The shadow of a smile played on his face, and he remained poised and mutely eloquent as if this were the moment toward which the entire service had been directed. This is how King Christophe must have looked when the dream of building the Citadel possessed him. This was Toussaint L'Ouverture when he swore to save his people from the yoke of oppression. This was Dessalines in whose bearing was the aloof pride of a conqueror. Majestically the *houngan* walked through the cleared space in the center of the chapel, paused a moment to nod to Reser and then moved to the altar. Here he bowed to a Higher Power and put down the sword.

With infinite care he began selecting several vials from among the altar furnishings. Then he began to work like a pharmacist compounding a prescription, putting into a large white mortar portions of cinnamon, nutmeg, cloves, anise and a variety of other tropical spices, all of which Reser identified. These were mixed together thoroughly, rhythmically to the beat of the drums. Then a *hounsi* carried the mortar to a spot near the tub.

Softly chanting a prayer Ti Cousin now sprinkled cologne and rum into the tub. He dipped his hand into the mortar and began to make the outline of a *veve* on the green water, letting the spices filter between his thumb and forefinger. Deftly he traced the patterns bringing about, as Reser explained, the synthesis of the *loa* and the worshipers. The *veve* was symbolic of the spirit of life moving on the face of the waters.

When the intricate design was finished and everyone's attention was focused on the tub the *houngan* intoned an invocation to Erzilie. This was followed by a litany to the *loa*. Then Ti Cousin returned to the altar and picked up the sword. On it he made a mystical sign with chalk, presented the sword to the four cardinal points and, with the drums booming, laid it across the tub. He signaled to a *hounsi,* and she set a small glass tumbler on the sword. Then she took a cup and filled the glass with the water of the sacred herbs.

I thought that this would be the moment for the sprinkling or baptizing of the children. I was never more mistaken. Amid the frenzy of the drums a chant arose, and the room exploded with emotion. Black hands reached out, struggling for the glass. A man got hold of it and raised it to his lips. Dimly in the swirling throng of faces and the reaching hands I remembered how Reser had told me that the people often struggled to touch the *veve*, to put their fingers upon it for special blessings. To drink it would be doubly efficacious.

Everyone was crowding into the center of the room. People were stretching their hands upward and outward, their bodies quivering, their faces ecstatic and their eyes half-closed, as the drums thrummed loud and fast.

I heard Lorena's excited whisper, "I must get a picture of this!"

"You can't!"

She managed to get up and started out. I followed her. In the confusion no one, not even Reser, seemed to notice us. The people were clamoring for the privilege of touching or drinking the water in the tub as if it were a holy sacrament. Perhaps it was. Would I ever know? Would I ever learn whether one draught could immunize me against sickness for the coming year or protect me from disease? Flattened against the wall by the dancing figures we made our way into the *tonnelle* and out into the dark plantation grounds. It was now midnight.

We walked in the direction of our car while the jangled voices of the worshipers formed a somber backdrop for our thoughts. Making our way to the *oto* we remembered that Lorena's camera equipment had been left on the porch at Ti Cousin's home. I asked Lorena to wait at the car, and taking her small flashlight I lighted my way through the path where earlier that night the candles had burned.

I crossed the dirt road and entered the *houngan's* yard. As I turned the corner of the house my light picked up the figure of a man standing. He wore torn trousers, an open shirt, a ripped-out hat. He was braiding strips of sisal. I turned the light away and walked past him with a whispered *"Bonsoir."* He made no reply. When I came out of the house he was gone.

As I started back to the *oto* a thought tormented me. For the first time in my years of research I felt myself an intruder spying upon the worship of a believing people. Were they not trying in their own way to come to terms with the mystery of their relation to the Infinite? Were they not also looking for the power and the presence of the Invisible Force behind their lives? What if their gods were not mine, their ritual not my ritual, their sacrifices not the kind I felt a man should offer? Who was I to say what their service should be? What if Voodoo to them was merely an escape from the drudgery and pain of a life that is often severe and hopeless?

I came to some sudden conclusions. Voodoo might well be lacking in high moral or ethical emphasis, but what was my standard of judgment? Upon what was I to base the morality or ethics of these people? Those whom I had met had no less a code by which to live and no less a philosophy to guide them than I. They had their standards, and on the level of their culture they lived by them. They had their faith, they loved the *loa,* they honored their priest.

These thoughts whirled in my mind on this fabulous Christmas Eve while the air was filled with the cacophony of the service.

I had been treated wonderfully well during my months in Haiti. The Voodooists were like all Haitians. They respected the *blanc.* They would say, "The *blanc* is unpredictable. He dresses strangely. He has queer habits. He does not know just what he believes. He is more interested in this world than in the next. He is mostly interested in money. There is much he needs to make him happy. He is always in a hurry. He is always restless. He lives as if someone were always after him. We do not understand his ways, but *le blanc* is always a great man. There is nothing *le blanc* can't do if he puts his hand to it. Everything progressive in Haiti has come from the *blanc Américain.*"

The drums never stopped. They called and commanded, "Come to *me,* come to *me,* come to *me!*" Reser's opinions were like words being spoken: "Voodoo is universal. It goes backward and forward, a link between the Infinite and the Known, between Cosmos and Man, between Primal Cause and Things to Come. It ties in with the Odyssey, with the Old Testament, with every holy book. It is Catholicism and Pentecostalism, Spiritualism and Faith Healing. It is a mystical order. Those on the outside will never know its secrets. Those on the inside will never tell."

I paused in the shadow of Ti Cousin's humble home. I looked up into the sky, wanting almost to believe on this holy night that every star was a *loa* and a *mystère.* I felt that I was touching the heart of Haiti, the Haiti that is in a state of awakening, the Haiti that no one can write about, the Haiti that is something that must be felt and breathed and smelled and experienced like the surge of an overwhelming love, like Voodoo—a thing of the spirit and a sensation.

I stood in the culture and environment of the Haitian peasant. I thought of the few pleasures and luxuries which he enjoyed. Though Reser always said the peasant's pleasures were many, I imagined they were only the pleasures of laughter and of the flesh and only the luxury of not being enslaved. I pictured the peasant working in the fields with his crude, impractical tools, carrying heavy burdens beneath the burning sun, walking at night with the gravel and dirt of the road bruising his bare feet. And I tried to think his thoughts after him. "There is no world but my world. I work all day and at night

I lay my aching back on the fiber mat. Who will help me? Where will I go? What can I do with my plot of ground? What is it I want? Why am I here?" And I heard his answer. "I have the *loa!* They are in the stars above and in the 'islands below the sea.' They are in the wind and at the crossroads, in nature and in the graves. They think as I think. They ask me to come and be as they are. They hint of magic and they work their miracles. They invite me to sing and dance and lose my-self in their possession. The drums help me to forget my life and remember them. The chanting sends sweet sensations through my body. The rattle of the *asson* reminds me of the world mysterious, the real world. This is Voodoo. It means so much to me that the first fruit of all I have is none too good for Damballa."

I saw a figure hurrying through the dark. Lorena called my name. "Here!" I said.

"Where have you been?" she asked. "Where's the camera?"

"Here it is."

"Listen to those drums!"

"Remember your promise to Reser."

"He surely won't object."

"Why not?

"He must realize what a terrific opportunity this is."

"Okay," I agreed and gave her the camera.

We went back to the *tonnelle* and stood at the door of the *hounfort* with a group of worshipers who looked at us curi-ously and eyed the camera. Were we going in? Why did we hesitate? These were questions I was asking myself. We were here to see not only the purification of the children, but also the

active participation of the only white man who had ever merited
the faith and favor of the Voodoo priesthood—the white man
with the dragon tattooed on his arm, an everlasting *veve* burned
into his flesh. He stood among the initiated. He knew how to
kill the sacrifices: pigs and turkeys for Petro, sheep and goats
and doves for the Rada *loa,* chickens for Damballa.

We watched in silent concentration. The white man in the
black setting held us enthralled. Then my gaze was drawn by
a power beyond my control. Ti Cousin stood within arm's
reach. I saw his eyes, and they were unlike any human eyes
that I had ever seen. They were luminous disks throwing off
aureoles of light. The group around me melted into the dark,
and Lorena and I stood half-hypnotized against our will. The
eyes seemed to draw deep down into the head and half bury
themselves inside the black sockets. The disks appeared to spin
and burn. What was he thinking? He could not speak to us,
nor we to him. The inevitable barrier of language held us apart.
But the eyes of Ti Cousin filled with a look of loneliness and
fatherly compassion. He seemed to be saying, Have you come
only to spy on us? What is it you want? Then he held out a
hand of welcome.

Lorena whispered, "Go on in. I'll put the camera back in the
car and be right with you." She hurried away.

I entered the *hounfort,* and Ti Cousin took me into an ante-
room, an inner sanctum about eight feet square. A large low
altar with the customary articles was lighted by floating wicks.

"*La chambre* Damballa," said Ti Cousin, and his voice recalled our visit to the room of Erzilie. He had been proud of
that shrine. He was proud of this and earnest in sharing it with

me. We went to the altar. He took from it an earthen jar and handed it to me. Graciously he asked me if I did not want to pay my respects to Damballa Wedo.

I took the jar awkwardly. I was wondering how to proceed when a voice behind me said, "Face the altar. Say an inward prayer of thanks for blessings received." Reser stood at the door, pleased and smiling. "Ask for continued help and guidance. Face the east and say, *'A table.'* Then face the west and say, *'D'abord.'* Face the north and say, *'Olandé.'* Face the south and say, *'Adonai.'* Starting at the opposite side from the basin pour three libations before the altar, one in the basin and three just outside the entrance door. Then kneel before the altar."

I obeyed. The sound of my voice in the little room reciting words that had more feeling than meaning for me filled me with the solemn reflection that Voodoo, like many other faiths, was as much a matter of the heart as of the mind. And as I went to my knees in front of Damballa's altar I tried once more to think the thoughts of the peasant who came to worship here. Prominently before me among the many primitive altar furnishings was a crucifix. Its purpose was ever the same, to engender the will to believe that God is near. In Damballa's chamber, primitive and crude as a manger, I had no doubt that faith had often been born for those who willed it so. Where were the witchcraft and black magic? Where the snake worship and cannibalism? The drums had stopped. The people were strangely quiet. I heard the soft cry of a child.

Looking up I saw Ti Cousin lifting a tiny black baby in his arms. I came to my feet. For an instant the old sensationalism of Voodoo sacrifices shot through my mind. But what was I seeing? Ti Cousin dipped a hand into the basin containing

some of the green aromatic mixture. He anointed the head and
body of the child with this sacred balm. Near him stood the
young parents. They watched intently and listened to the whispered ritual, satisfied that their child was being set apart for
special protection for the coming year.

In the doorway mothers were waiting with their children.
This was a christening ceremony of the kind one might find
almost anywhere in the Christian world. Reser came to tell me
that it would continue throughout the night.

But even now the banging of the drums was starting again in
the chapel, hands were clapping, bare feet were rhythmically
pounding the floor, voices were shouting jubilantly and freely.
Soon the *loa* would sweep down upon someone strongly in
possession. Soon the personality would change, and the gods
would reign.

This was Voodoo, and what was I to say?

Chapter 6

THE DAYS IMMEDIATELY FOLLOW-
ing Christmas are important in the calendar of Voodoo lore.
They were important to us, too—especially Epiphany, January
6, for it was on this morning that I arose early to prepare for a
trip out of town only to stagger groggily back to bed.

Lorena's alarmed "What's the matter?" was my cue for a
confession. Ever since Christmas Eve I had been fighting a feeling of ennui or something distantly related to nervous exhaus-
tion. I had been dragging myself to Voodoo services and
wearily following Lorena on her untiring photographic jaunts.
Just the day before, during a long interview with the dancer
Destiné, I had the feeling of near collapse. This was it.

Lorena stuck a fever thermometer into my mouth and began
digging in a suitcase for the aspirin. By the time she found it
the thermometer was ready for the reading. Through moist
eyes I saw the result in her horrified expression.

"You need a doctor." And off she went down to the lobby
telephone.

I was too weak to resist. This had never happened to me
before, and I was unable to cope even mentally with the circumstances.

Lorena returned and reported, "The phone is out of order again. Take these." She insisted that I swallow a couple of aspirin, then laid a cold cloth on my forehead.

"I'll be right back," she said. "They say there's an M. D. a few blocks from here."

Through a feverish mist I saw her go. While struggling for some explanation of what had hit me I heard the door open slowly. I raised myself with effort as Ariette the maid cautiously peered in. Her face was haunting black against the white door, her eyes looked at me with solemn concern. "You *seeck?*" she asked.

"I feel pretty sick," I told her.

She was in the room now with a hand on the doorknob. She raised herself on tiptoe to see me better.

In a voice of terror cushioned against a tremor of surprise she said a single word, "*Wanga!*" She meant, Who put a hex on you?

This did not make me feel any better. My own words had returned to torment me, for I had often joked with Ariette and the houseboy Espere about hexes and *wangas* and superstitions among the people I had met.

"*Wanga,*" I said weakly and heard the door close.

Wanga! It was a fearsome word to drive into my consciousness at such a moment, and dreamily I remembered that there was also a letter among my effects which said, "Don't go to Haiti! Voodoo is witchcraft and black magic!" I think I groaned. I was burning with fever.

I had sensations of falling in space. I thought I heard a drum. In a foggy way I dreamed about Reser. Reser had no telephone. Reser did not know about our plans for the trip out of town.

Where was Reser? Who was he? How well did I know him? I pondered on libations to Damballa. I dreamed of sacrifices. *Wangas* floated in my mind. I thought I heard a drum.

The sounds were footsteps coming up the stairs. Lorena seemed unreal as she moved into the room. She was a shadow. Her voice was one of those I had heard long ago, a voice that came from behind a curtain, from an "island below the sea," an unreal voice, but it came closer and she bent over me.

"I couldn't get a doctor," her voice said. "That is, I couldn't get the one that they told me about. I called Pastor McConnell, the Methodist missionary. He said he would get one and have him come right over. How are you now?"

"Hot," I said.

It must have been some thirty minutes later that the fever broke. For a moment Lorena and the objects in the room cleared. Then it came again—the burning sensation and the violent pressure on the solar plexus. More aspirin, more cold packs, more *wangas* and more drums.

Dr. Carl Wilhelm Lemke came into the room. The stairs had been hard on him. He was an elderly man and he was panting. Through the haze of fever, confusion and pain I heard his voice—one I shall never forget.

"So, what's the matter?" He took my hand and counted my pulse. Gently he asked, "Have you been out in the hills—in the swamps?"

I nodded.

"Have you ever had malaria?"

I shook my head.

"You've got it now." And I saw him open his little black bag.

I had it, and evidently Dr. Lemke, a German who had been

in the tropics for thirty-three years, knew how to deal with it. As he prepared to give me a shot of Aralen, I heard him ask, "Didn't you take any preventive medicine? Don't you have any paludrine?"

"We have some of these," Lorena said and showed him the bottle which Reser had given us long ago. It seemed a thousand years ago and in an altogether different world that I had heard Reser say, "If we're going out together, take three of these a week. Regularly."

"Yes." It was Dr. Lemke's voice. "Those are very good. You didn't take them?" He was talking to me. I shook my head. I heard the old man sigh. "I could ask why you didn't take them, but that would not help matters now. Turn over."

Turn over. I was to hear those two words many times during the next few days! Dr. Lemke was in charge and my idiosyncrasies about pill-taking bowed to medical authority and scientific skill. He called Lorena to his office on the following day to show her the blood smears under the miscroscope and to tell her that mine was a bad case.

"How a man can come down here and run into a mosquito as big as this one," he said, "is beyond me."

For this type of malaria he knew the timetable like an expert. "Tomorrow the fever will still be high—a hundred and four. The pain in the stomach will be somewhat better. By Wednesday the fever should be down. But it will fluctuate. Call me if his feeling of nausea gets worse."

There were the usual orders: a darkened room, the cycle of medicines, liquids, no visitors and so on. But he did not prepare me for the first night of delirium when my throat was burning and I could not get hold of an ice-cold drink of fellowship! Nor did he predict that I would spend hours endlessly weigh-

ing the respective merits of Voodoo and Christianity until I had
all the *loa* and all the saints arrayed against one another and
against me. Nor that I would walk back and forth to the "island
below the sea" arm in arm with Agué, or dream about Erzilie,
or talk to Damballa, or, most of all, contemplate in a medley
of disjointed philosophical concepts the possibility of dying on
the Enchanted Isle.

Through the eternity of befuddled hours I wondered why not
one of us who believe in saints or *loa* is in a hurry to become
one. Why, even though we boast about the beauty and perfec-
tion of the world beyond, do we cling with all our might—
down to the last capsule—to this present world? Foggily I came
to the conclusion that it must be easier to die as a Voodooist than
as one of our so-called cultured Christians for this reason: the
Voodooist lives much closer to our mutual Mother, the Earth.
He belongs to that enviable society which has the courage and
the will to walk barefoot and feel the magnetism of the earth,
something which Christians have been out of contact with
for nearly two thousand years. The Voodooist sits, squats
and sleeps on the ground from childhood and has a sense of
being a part of nature. He is born on the ground and nourished
on the ground and on the ground he is content to die. The
earth made him, and it is only natural that he should return to
it easily and without care.

Whatever he does in life, he does in partnership with the
land. He builds his home out of the things of the land. He
gets his food from the land. The objects on his altar, all the
way from the magic stones to the equally magic jars, are scooped
up from the land. His much-honored deity, Damballa, is sym-
bolized by the creature that crawls on its belly on the land.

There is nothing that his Mother, the Earth, does not know, and he knows his Mother. He understands the secrets of the herbs she gives for healing and the herbs she gives for death. He knows what he can expect from her in the way of help or harm. He knows her moods, her wishes and her rhythm. That is one reason why the Voodooist feels he knows the great Saint Jesus so well. That Gran Mait preached while seated on the ground. He went into the wilderness during His retreats and He had no place but the earth upon which to lay His head. That is why the Voodooists can best understand the agony of that Man's death. He was forced to die without the solacing touch of the earth, lifted up in space, forsaken and alone.

And I decided it was unfair for us to judge the Voodooist until we actually put ourselves in his place and understood his relationship to the earth. For our life was no longer a part of the land. Our religion had the Gran Mait going first class in planes and trains and driving His own expensive *oto*. We worshiped Him in churches, the splendor of which could only embarrass Him, and we treated Him as if He had been born in our culture and in our time. We failed even to understand the symbols He used because they were no longer a part of our experience. Actually He lived more like a peasant than like one of the elite and when He died He was buried in a sepulcher that was more like a *houngan's* tomb than a Christian's grave.

This the fever did to me. And since this was Haiti, I felt I could have faced death more easily had I been a Voodooist.

Days were marked by the honking of horns, the cries of the vendors and the tap of the bootblack's box. Nights brought the barking of dogs, the crowing of cocks in the moonlight and the murmur of drums. There was also another sound, soothing, productive: Lorena developing films in her wardrobe dark-room. The squeak of the tank was reassuring and there was always the thrill afterward of examining the dripping scenes.

An American newspaperman stopped at the hotel one day and came up to the room. I was feeling better by then and joked with him about the aberrations I had in thinking that a *wanga* had been pinned on me. He snapped his fingers with a great idea and whipped out a notebook.

"Lay off," I said weakly. "The only thing that was put on me was a mosquito bite out in some swamp."

"Sure," he agreed, "but why should that one malaria-packing mosquito pick you? The *wanga!* 'Voodoo research backfires. . . . Voodoo curse follows investigator. . . . Black magic too much for white explorer.' It's great! Everybody who has ever heard of Voodoo expects something like this. Everybody who has ever heard of Haiti thinks this is exactly what ought to happen."

"No comment," I said.

"How about the whole story?" he urged.

"Here it is," I told him. "I didn't take the little white pills." That thought was always enough to bring back the fever.

The days passed, with time measured by a diet stepped up gradually from Gerber's baby food to Haitian stew, by less and less temperature-reading and by fewer visits from the valorous Dr. Lemke, who had become an immortal friend. Pastor Mc-Connell and other Port-au-Princians frequently dropped around, but the one man I wanted most to see remained mysteriously absent. I progressed from bed to chaise lounge at the window, from bedroom to breezeway, but there was no sign or sound of *M'sieur* Doc.

2.

THEN on my third visit to the veranda, from where one catches the gateway view of the pageantry of the Champs de Mars, a familiar "Oh-o!" greeted me, and the buoyant figure of the invincible white Haitian came swinging up the steps.

"*Kouma ou ye?*" he asked with a laugh, as the arm with the dragon went affectionately around my shoulders.

I answered in Creole that I was fine.

"Ah!" he said. "Now I see what you have been doing during your convalescence—learning the language. *Bon! Bon!*"

"How did you know I was convalescing?" I asked. "You didn't even know I was sick."

"What! I knew *all* about it—temperature a hundred and five, shots of Aralen, Gerber's baby food!"

"Darn your Voodoo!" I said.

"No Voodoo," he answered, amused. "I was here."

"In spirit?"

"In the flesh. Didn't they tell you? I was here and was told you were sick."

"Why didn't you come up?"

"You had a good doctor. Furthermore, I made it a practice long ago not to call on sick people unless they ask me to come. It doesn't help them and it doesn't do me any good."

I liked him for that. He was thoroughly honest about it, and when Lorena came down he repeated his sentiment to her.

She agreed with his point of view but said, "I really needed you. We thought it might have been a *wanga.*"

"It probably was," he said, "but not the kind you think. One of Marc's own making. Made by his refusal to take the preventive medicine I gave you. *You* took it, didn't you?"

"Of course," said Lorena. "And you are right. I took the pills. He didn't. Now he takes not three a week but three a day."

"We have a proverb," the white man said. *"Ce moune malade qui connai valeur remede.* . . . It is the sick who know the value of the medicine."

On this we had a drink mixed for us by the houseboy Espere, a *ponche citron* with the traditional circle of sugar clinging to a thin film of lime juice around the rim of the glass.

"I hear," Reser said, "you are planning to leave tomorrow."

"That's right."

"Why not stay a while longer? There are some interesting services coming up."

"My hard luck," I admitted. "My schedule says I must be back in February."

"Next time take off all year and follow Voodoo around the calendar."

"Will you still be here?"

"I'll always be here," he said.

"Wouldn't you like to come back to the States?" asked Lorena.

"I'd like to come for a visit. But never to stay."

"Don't you feel you owe America something?" I asked.

"I gave half of my life to my country," he replied, referring to his record of service in the United States Navy. "I feel justified in traveling the rest of the road in my own way. My children are grown up, married, well taken care of. Their future is assured. My three grandchildren love me, and I love them. But neither they nor their parents actually need me. They are self-sufficient, as most people in the States seem to be. It is different with my friends in Haiti. They need me. My job down here is not done. Anything I can do for Haiti, I want to do. The pearl of great price holds me here."

"And Voodoo's strange altars," I added.

"They are not so strange," he corrected as he gazed out across the plaza where the black people moved with their rhythmic stride across the Champs de Mars. Color, movement and the symphony of sounds never ceased, and the sunlight was purest white.

"You've been sick," Reser said to me, "and Lorena nursed you back to health. There was a time when my son also lay at the point of death here in Port-au-Prince. He had been working for an engineering company bucking a pneumatic drill in a tunnel at Carrefour. When his shift was over at midnight he imprudently bared his overheated body to the cool mountain breeze. He ended up with lobar pneumonia. I engaged a Harvard-educated Haitian physician who treated him with all the skill that could be asked of any doctor. In spite of this, he got steadily worse. His temperature shot up to a hundred and five and practically stayed there."

He said to Lorena, "You know what I went through. For days and days my son was delirious. The doctor had ordered ice-water sponge baths every thirty minutes. Three devoted Haitian women attended to this and never left his bedside. But he could take no nourishment, no liquids. Not even a spoonful of ice

water. He was rapidly becoming dehydrated, and I was help-
less. Then in his semiconscious babbling he murmured, 'Melon,
melon.' Teaspoonful by teaspoonful every few minutes, hour
after hour, these women fed him the juice of melons. The
precious fluid kept the breath of life in his body. Day and night
these blessed women nursed him back to health. The result was
that he overcame death to become one of the nationally known
American heroes of World War II. So you see, that, too, has
drawn my roots deeper into this soil."

"Does your son ever come down here?" asked Lorena.

"Occasionally. He flies with Pan American. Both he and my
daughter speak Creole fluently. They know Haiti. Outsiders
don't know this land or the people. There is something here
that cannot be seen with the eyes or understood with the mind.
I'll tell you what it is. I'll tell you the great secret of the Haitian
peasant. Each soul feels and knows itself to be immortal. It
feels and knows that the entire universe with all its goodness
and greatness and beauty is for it and belongs to it forever." He
said this as if it were his *fait accompli,* entrusted to me only
now that our parting was near, as if he sensed that I was at last
able to understand.

"These peasants never heard of the philosopher Lecomte du
Noüy, but they know instinctively the truth of what he said
about a design and purpose in life. They have no idea who the
German dramatist Lessing was, but they use his words when
they say, 'Why should I worry about missing something? Is
not all eternity mine?' Spinoza to them is not even a name, but
they know better than he that everything that exists is a manifestation of God."

The champion of the black people of the Enchanted Isle was having his say. It was Reser, the many-sided personality speaking, and his words were those of Ti Cousin and Ti Toma, of Voodoo priest and Voodoo worshiper.

"I claim," he announced, "that there is a higher faculty than reason through which one comes to know God. Gifted men who have given us insight into the infinite have vibrated in harmony with cosmic life. I believe that our world in its never-ending flight passes through spatial fields and that the people who are in tune with these fields, be they wise or otherwise, become the recipients of great revelations."

He paused a moment, then continued, "When you consider that this old world of ours has been going in four directions at once since the beginning of time you will agree that we have gone through quite a bit of space. Our axial speed is a thousand miles per hour. Our orbital speed around the sun is eighteen miles per second. The solar system is on its way toward a point in the constellation Hercules at the rate of twelve miles per second, and our whole galaxy is rotating at a speed of one hundred and seventy-five miles per second. This I once told a peasant working with his oxen in the sugar-cane field. Do you know what he said? 'What is so wonderful about that? Aren't you talking about our *Gran Mait?*'"

He got up abruptly. "On this note," he said, "we should have started our Haitian visit, not ended it!" He held out a hand to Lorena. "So," he said, affectionately calling her by name, "*bon voyage.*" Then turning to me he crossed his wrists, and we shook hands three times Voodoo-style, after which he said, "Haiti is called *le pays du revenants*—the country of those who come back. May the saints, the *loa* and the *mystères* watch over and guide you until you, too, are *revenants*."

With this he walked quickly down the pathway, through the gate and into the street without looking back. At the edge of the plaza we saw him raise a hand in greeting to a peasant friend and heard his laughing *"Ai-yai-yai!"*

Reser passed out of our sight but not out of our minds. We thought of him when we packed our bags and put in the Voodoo articles: an *asson,* a string of *hounsi* beads, a few *paquets,* a small drum and several altar pieces. We spoke of him when Lorena methodically put her rolls of undeveloped film and her envelopes of processed negatives into the crocodile case.

Also packed as gifts in our going-home parcels were some sisal mats made for us by Ti Toma and a portfolio of songs. These compositions, words and music, nearly a hundred in number, were the published works of Dr. Carl Wilhelm Lemke, which he insisted I should have.

Missionary McConnell came with his *oto* the following morning to take us to the airport. He had a story to tell us of the need for American dollars to help the Protestant work. He pleaded with us to take home the entreaty that Christianity desperately needs help to fight the Voodoo gods. He had a good, strong argument, and it was backed by many years of service.

Later, as I looked down over the wings of the rising plane, the battle of faiths seemed wholly irrelevant. The cathedral and the cemetery, the palace and the plaza, *hounfort* and chapel were already toyland settings. Haiti was merely another thought of the *Gran Mait* flung into space.

How small this thought seemed and yet how infinite! How

simple it all was, yet how complex. How much human blood
had washed those wooded hills to win liberty for a tortured race,
and how many drums had beat to make a people free! *Wangas*
and crosses, *houngans* and priests, Saint Jesus and Damballa all
had had a part in it.

I felt cold. Lorena wrapped a blanket around me. I began
to perspire. Dr. Lemke's last words—"You are in no condition
to go home"—came back to me. I glanced down at the white
fingers of the Windward Passage snapping up from the deep
blue. I thought of Agué. Who could forget the dramatic songs
that honored Agué with their rhythmic *Chung! Chung!* in im-
itation of the crash of waves on the shore or the boom of the
cannon on warships and pirate ships off Tortuga? Who could
ever erase from his mind the pictures of the Voodoo god of the
sea as he sat on a small stool for a boat and rowed around with
two canes for oars? I thought of him and said a little prayer,
"Carry us safely, Agué, carry us well!" The *loa* answered in the
soothing drone of the motor, telling me that all I needed was
paludrine and time.

Lorena checked over her record of pictures and decided that
she could put her camera away until we picked up our car in
Camagüey, Cuba. So we sat back and enjoyed the trip.

On the following day we drove from Camagüey to Havana
where we had a reservation at the Packard Hotel. We arrived
there late at night, which was according to schedule. The room
had been held for us, which I thought was a good sign. In fact,
everything was favorable, even to the reading of the fever thermometer. Contentedly we opened the windows of our room to
the shadowy outline of Morro Castle and went to sleep.

3.

IN THE morning when we awoke the Castle was already a sunlit sentinel in the Bay of Havana. Lorena went down to get the three-a-day paludrine pills from the car. I stood at our third-story window and looked out over the Malecon, Havana's famed ocean drive. The waves were tossing their white spray theatrically across the breakwater. In the park near the monument of Gral Gomez a flower vendor was setting up his display. Lines of cars were turning steadily into the Prado, the laurel-shaded boulevard. My attention was drawn from these tourist-folder scenes to our parked car. Lorena had stopped abruptly. She drew back. Then I saw her open the car door cautiously, reach in, close it and walk back across the street.

When she returned to the room she reported, "Somebody tried to break into the car last night. The ventilator window is smashed, but they didn't get in. Everything seems to be in place. Here is the paludrine and here is your shaving kit which was on the seat."

I looked out at the car once more, and through its windows I could see the Haitian baskets which were piled high on the back seat. These assured me, too, that everything was intact.

When we went down to the car, however, I said to Lorena, "They did get in. I had a suit draped over these baskets, and the suit is gone."

A look of terror came into Lorena's eyes. She threw back the front seat and plunged her hands in frantically among the closely-packed bags. Feverishly she set aside boxes, baskets and suitcases, one after the other, and ended her search with a cry of pain.

"You know what else is gone?" she said, and her frenzied actions had already told me all too well what was implied. "The suitcase with my crocodile case!"

We could not bring ourselves to say, "The pictures and the films," but after a methodical check throughout the car Lorena sat stunned, looking blankly into space.

"It's all gone," she said incredulously. "The negatives, the eighty rolls of black and white, the rolls of color. All gone."

There was almost nothing I could say. The frightful discovery cut as deeply into my feelings as into hers. She was too defeated to cry. She could only repeat, "It can't be! It just can't be!"

I knew what she was thinking: her first research trip with me—her days of adventuring—her *"Quitte um tiré portré ou"*—her portraits of Haitian people—the life and moods that she had caught—her months of picture taking—nights of developing in her wardrobe darkroom. . . .

There was something else. I felt it. She felt it. We could not talk of it, for it was too mysterious, too fantastic. But we thought about it as we sat in the midst of a tragic experience. Our minds were crowded to the breaking point with Voodoo: the *mambo* letting the meal filter between her forefinger and thumb, the zombi, the *houngan,* the *hounsi,* the drums, the sacrifices, *l'kabrit,* Damballa, Erzilie Freda, Agué and a white man moving familiarly through the scenes. What was it he had once said? "I photograph these scenes in my mind. No one can steal them from me, and I offend no one that way." While

Lorena sat at the steering wheel with her head in her arms and I stood beside the car on this Havana street the long arm of a Voodoo *wanga* reached out and touched me lightly on the shoulder.

"Come on," I said.

There followed the usual heartbreaking routine. We reported the theft to the Cuban police, the impervious, unfeeling police who took it as a commonplace that anyone who neglected to take everything out of the car should expect to be victimized. The Cuban Tourist Bureau passed the word from desk to desk with a shrug of despair. "Why didn't you take something as valuable as this to your room?" they asked. It was as difficult for them to understand as it was for us to explain that we had been too tired and I too sick to take the necessary precautions which one must take in Cuba's capital city.

Our complaint to the manager of the Packard Hotel was met with stubborn rebuff. "What if the hotel boy did assure you that the car would be all right? We are not responsible for what he says. What if the elevator man did say that things would be safe? What does he know? This is *Habana!*"

We reported the loss to the American Embassy. We ran ads offering rewards. We alerted the camera shops and talked and pleaded with policemen on their beats. For all of this we got nothing but the stock reply, "These things happen all the time."

We would never have abandoned the search but for a schedule in the States which had to be met. We made a final tour of camera shops and police headquarters. Then, leaving the matter in the hands of Cuban officials, we took the boat to Miami. Here we told our story to the FBI before reluctantly starting our homeward trek.

Although hoping against hope that the pictures would be recovered, I was tormented by a feeling of awful finality. Hope was blotted out by a haunting superstition that mere man could do nothing. On our first night out I wrote Reser in detail about the theft. Already across the miles I seemed to hear his arresting "Oh-o!" The impression almost made me want to return to Haiti to learn his reaction and his analysis of this circumstance. In fact, as the distance between us increased and the days went by the loss became more and more ironical.

It was now February and, even though we ran into blizzard conditions, I had to accept the probability that, somewhere in the tropical fastness of the Enchanted Isle, Reser was even now beating out a Voodoo rhythm on the taut goatskin of a sacred drum. Or maybe he was gazing into a glass of water or into a crystal ball and already seeing the details of all that we had gone through. If so, could he not also tell us clairvoyantly what had happened to the crocodile case and how the film could be recovered? Surely the *loa* knew. And surely Reser was sufficiently near to them to get them to tell!

These thoughts kindled hope in me, and I ventured to say to Lorena that by the time I had my Voodoo notes in shape the film might be found and the pictures used in the publication. We carried this encouragement with us to the very streets of our home town. I was absorbed with it when I went to the post office and picked up the packages of mail that had accumulated. There was not a word from Havana, but among the letters was a special delivery *par avion* envelope which I seized upon eagerly. It was from Reser, and I tore it open and glanced at the contents, then reread it slowly from the affectionate *"Trés cher* Marc" all the way to the *"Toujours votre."*

The message read: "Shocked and heartbroken at your report of the Havana theft. What can I say? One thing, the scenes and the people will always be here. Why not come back, camera and all, and try all over again?"

I showed the letter to Lorena. Bundled in our coats we sat in our cold house reading through the mail, always coming back to Reser's note.

Lorena lingered over a folder in her hand. "Here," she said, "is a great bargain in new film just my size. I'm ordering ten cartons."

"For a Voodoo venture?" I asked.

"Why not?" It was a good question. The lure of Haiti had crept into our hearts and again I heard a still, small voice like the *loa* calling, "Come to *me,* come to *me,* come to *me!*"